What people are saying about
All You Need Is HART!

All You Need Is HART! is an instruction manual for life! It is a path to happiness that we are all looking for. HART has transformed me, and I would recommend this to everyone who is searching for real happiness.

I have learned through HART that the only way we can be happy is by resolving our own issues before others and that the essence of life is love. I am deeply honored and grateful to meet Helene and experience HART.

Thank you, Helene, for being who you are. It has encouraged me to be who I am.

—Simmi Zaveri, Computer Engineer

I believe that Helene Rothschild's book, **All You Need Is HART!**, should be essential reading for everyone from teen years onwards. It deals in a simple, practical way with all the issues that can confront or challenge a person. It is written with love and is easy to read. This book allows the reader to get in touch immediately with their inner child and to cancel any destructive qualities within it such as anger, guilt or rebellion.

I thoroughly enjoyed reading and working with it. I have no hesitation in recommending it thoroughly to all those who wish to change negative traits to positive ones. We all need such help. Why not avail yourself of it now?

—Joana McCutcheon, Retired Architect

I have worked with Helene and her HART therapy and it has truly transformed my life. I highly recommend that you embrace this book, for it will change your life too, in so many meaningful and profound ways. Thank you, Helene!

—Minna Andersen-Zimmer, Print Editor

All You Need Is HART! takes you straight to where personal growth and development happens. And it does so with clarity, insightfulness, and compassion for those seeking life changes.
–Cynthia Warger, PHD

Your book is wonderful, Helene. It is clear, constructive, enormously helpful, and inspirational. It is a credit to you. I know it has the power to assist many thousands (and more) of people.
–Shirley Lovell, Homeopath and Naturopath

What people have said about Helene's insights and solutions in her previous book, **Free to Fly—Dare to be a Success**, Helene Rothschild has found the way...and it works!
–Actress Kim Novak

Creative power...the authors wake up this powerful resource and show how effectively it can be used.
–Virginia Satir,
author of **People Making and Making Contact**

If you want to root out self-defeating core beliefs that keep you from feeling successful in your life, you'll benefit from **Free To Fly—Dare To Be A Success**.
–Ken Keyes, Jr.,
author of **Handbook to Higher Consciousness**

Free To Fly provides seekers a delightful choice of practical, inspiring and effective techniques toward healthier relationships and individual growth.
–Assemblyman John Vasconcellos

HART Testimonials

I know of no other counseling system or technique where I could have accomplished so much in so little time.

– B.S., CA

I have had the good fortune of meeting Helene and receiving HART sessions. The process has enabled me to move past invisible limitations that continually blocked my success. I am grateful that Helene has perfected the art of success.

– R. W., AZ

I have been working with Helene and the HART process, and I have felt a profound sense of change within me; physically, emotionally, and spiritually. By using Helene's process I have come to understand that it is our birthright to live in joy and in peace.

– M.Z., IN

To my surprise, Helene helped me in five minutes overcome my phone phobia that I have been suffering with for 42 years. Needless to say, I am very grateful!

– K. S., AZ

My visits with Helene were literally inspiring and effective. I saw her three times, and she guided me through a whole bunch of muck and helped me heal. She has been an important factor in my inner development. Thank you, Helene, and keep on helping others; it is awesome!

– M.O., CA

Great burdens have been lifted from my wife and me. In just thirty minutes your insights helped us make sense of our lives and enabled us to release the pain that was dragging us down. We've found a new source of wisdom and strength within ourselves. Our marriage has also grown closer—more compassionate and more patient. Thanks again!

– E. M., CO

After one session I was no longer diagnosed with early-onset Parkinson's Disease. Thank you Helene also for helping me know and feel that I can be healed, and strength can be gained from shedding old wounds and self-blame. You have great insight and understanding!

– L. M., IN

Based on a blood test, the doctor was concerned about my liver. After you helped me clear my anger, my ultrasound came back perfectly normal.

– G.M., AZ

After our wonderful session, I felt so super. Thank you! Spirit has entrusted you with such wonderful gifts. My hay fever was so bad that I was ready to go to the Emergency Room. But after the half-hour phone session my sinuses felt better, and the next day I could hear better that I have in a long, long time.

– A. W., Alaska

My processes with you, Helene, were enlightening, comforting, and revealed much of my inner being to me. It was more than incredible; it was expanding. Bless you!

– J. K., WA

Thank you Helene for all your help, love, wisdom, brilliance, experience and the willingness to keep learning. Thank you for your sincere desire to see people free.

– D.G., AZ

Helene has saved my life, literally. When I first met her I had very low self-esteem. Through listening to her personal growth tapes and having sessions with her, I now have the confidence to do anything I want. Helene has the ability to intuitively know what to say in order to get to the root issue and let it go completely on all levels of your beingness. I am truly grateful that I am now living in a conscious and meaningful way. Thank you Helene

– B.M., CA

After the first half hour session with Helene, I awoke the next morning with my neck so strong that I stopped having to go to the chiropractor. After the second session, all my bones – my hands, feet, and spine – were straightened out. It was a miracle! Thank you a million times.

– S.F., CA

Helene, after our amazing half-hour phone session, I felt like I had received a heavy acupuncture treatment. My spiking fevers stopped. My physical therapist said, "You look like you are in love. You seem to be glowing. You aren't so congested and your muscles are more relaxed. Even your range of motion has improved. Something is very different!" Thank you from the center of my heart. I hope that you will continue to share your gifts.

– M. B., CA

After a half-hour session my bleeding hemorrhoids were gone—truly a miracle. Thank you!

– J.T., AZ

The two thirty-minute telephone-counseling sessions I had with Helene Rothschild were life transforming. Even after many years of therapy, I was experiencing difficulties in my work and interpersonal relationships. Issues related to being adopted, my family of origin, and three failed marriages were creating conflicts for me. Helene was able to clear away all of the debris from past wounds and decisions in these two short sessions. She assisted me in discovering where blockage existed; and in a supportive, safe, and loving way, she allowed me to release years of pain. I am very grateful for the many gifts she possesses and for her willingness to share these gifts so abundantly.

– M.M., AZ

Thank you for the tools to forge a life-long, loving relationship. That is truly a gift of a lifetime.

– D.K, NY

All You Need Is
HART!

Create Love, Joy, and Abundance – NOW!

by
Helene Rothschild

Robert D. Reed Publishers • Bandon, OR

Robert D. Reed Publishers
P.O. Box 1992
Bandon, OR 97411
Phone: 541-347-9882 • Fax: -9883
E-mail: 4bobreed@msn.com
web site: www.rdrpublishers.com

Typesetter: **Barbara Kruger**
Cover: **Cleone Lyvonne** and **Grant Prescott**

ISBN 1-931741-72-7
ISBN 978-1-931741-72-9

Library of Congress Control Number 2006900414

Manufactured, typeset and printed in the United States of America

Disclaimer: The information and exercises in this book are not
intended to replace medical or psychiatric care. If you are working with
doctors or mental health professionals, you are advised to consult with
them. The author or publisher has neither liability nor responsibility
to any person or entity with respect to any problems allegedly caused,
directly or indirectly, by the information in this book.

Dedicated to assisting you

To "Love Yourself to Peace"

The key to health, happiness,

Success, and world peace.

Acknowledgments

I would like to express my deepest appreciation to the following people:

My clients, for your courage to face your fears, for trusting me to help you heal yourself, and for all that you have taught me as we journeyed together on your growth path.

My students, for allowing me to assist you in your personal and professional growth, and for your courage and determination to go right to the core with your clients.

My friends and loved ones, for encouraging and supporting me in my life mission.

My many teachers, for sharing your experiences and wisdom with me.

My editors, Cleone Lyvonne, Minna Andersen-Zimmer, Shirley Lovell, Simmi Zaveri, Joana McCutcheon, and Diane Goulder, for your time, energy, support, and valuable feedback.

My publisher, Robert D. Reed, for recognizing the value of what I have learned and written, and assisting me to offer it to the public.

Love, Helene Rothschild

Contents

Introduction

HART: Holistic And Rapid Transformation

Are you ready to be happier, healthier, and more successful in every area of your life? With this empowering handbook, you can create the life you desire. The keys to fulfillment are in your hands. There is no need to search out there for answers anymore—they are inside of you!

As a Marriage, Family Therapist for over 26 years, I have had the wonderful opportunity to make a difference in many people's lives. Men, women, and children resolved their issues, learned how to communicate constructively, experienced more happiness and success, and improved their health and relationships.

My clients taught me that we are unique, but our problems are not. They also enlightened me about the causes of our problems, our human dramas. Because of our negative beliefs about others, the world, and ourselves, our chances for happiness seem locked up, out of our reach.

With the goal of helping people overcome their blocks as quickly and as efficiently as I could, I developed a process I call HART: Holistic and Rapid Transformation (previously known as Creative Therapy). Like a private detective, I diligently searched for the negative decisions that were keeping the clients in the illusion that they were not okay. Through the HART process, they were able to replace the hurtful negative thoughts with positive ones.

The results were quick and transformational. In many cases, clients had instant results. For example, Susan, an intelligent, attractive 38-year-old blonde, came to me because she was struggling financially, and she was unsuccessful in her job search. I helped her uncover her self-sabotaging beliefs and change them to positive ones.

After the session, Susan drove the short distance to her apartment and was welcomed by a wonderful surprise. There was a phone message on her answering machine about a job offer that had been recorded during the time she was on her way home. Susan phoned me, filled with excitement and disbelief. I congratulated her and then said, "This is a wonderful example of how powerful your thoughts are in creating your reality".

Through the HART process, many clients discovered how their negative thoughts even caused their illnesses and accidents. As a result, they were often able to experience immediate improvement in their bodies.

For example, Mary, a 45-year-old accountant, told me she was diagnosed by her neurosurgeon with early onset Parkinson's disease. We did a half-hour phone session because she was living in a different state. Through the HART process, I helped Mary release painful decisions she had made about relationships. The following week, I received an exciting email. Mary wrote that the perplexed neurosurgeon said that there were no longer any signs of the early symptoms of the disease.

There are many more fascinating examples in this book about men and women who were able to change their lives as they altered their beliefs. There are also numerous insights and solutions to help you create the health, happiness, and success that you desire and deserve.

One of my students once said, "Helene, HART is more than a healing process; it is a way of life!" Her wise words rang true for many people, including me. The basic principles can apply to any situation. Once you understand them, you can have a different perception of others, the world, and yourself. Your life is then likely to transform like a caterpillar becoming a butterfly. You can feel free to spread your wings, do what you choose, and be all that you are.

Life is so much easier and more fun when you have a "Manual for Life". You can continue to read and work with the invaluable insights and solutions, and reach higher levels of personal and professional success. I suggest that you purchase a notebook in which to do the exercises. This way you can repeat the processes and receive even more answers to whatever you want to explore. Remember that all the wisdom you need is inside of you!

However you choose to benefit from this book, it is helpful to be patient and persevering. Keep your sense of humor and enjoy the journey called life!

Part I

Right To The Core
With H A R T

Chapter 1

All You Need Is H A R T !

You really can create love, joy, and abundance now! You do have what it takes to reach your desired goals. These can also be your success stories.

When Glen realized the truth about commitment, it no longer frightened him and he was finally willing to ask Sherry to marry him. Cindy's life was much more fun after she overcame her negative thoughts about playing. Steve found himself more at ease at work and at home when he realized he could simply demonstrate his love and skills—he did not have to try to prove himself. Judy overcame her fear of intimacy and is enjoying her new partner. Jan and Bob had a happier marriage and family when they began to understand what their children wanted and needed, improved their communication skills, and learned how to solve their problems. Karen and David decided to stay in their marriage after they resolved their personal and couple issues.

Barry and Lynn overcame their fears of success and were able to follow their dreams. Katherine finally won the "battle of the bulge" and easily maintained her desired weight. Kevin released his negative issues about money and was promoted to a higher paying position.

When Mary identified and released the negative beliefs that caused her to hurt her knee, she avoided an operation. Jennifer's back felt great after she released her stored anger constructively.

The HART process can also help you enjoy health, happiness, and success. Now is the time to create the reality you desire.

The following two chapters will explain the basic HART process. The information, case studies, and exercises in Parts II and III are designed to help you experience Holistic and Rapid Transformation. Enjoy the fascinating journey of self-empowerment!

Chapter 2

Basic Principles

*H*ow did the HART process come about? While I was studying for a Masters Degree in Counseling, I somehow naturally started to develop my own therapeutic process. I imagined a puzzle and saw some missing pieces. Over the course of a few years, the spaces were filled and HART was created.

My clients were experiencing great success, and I could not accommodate all the people who requested my services. One day I decided to start writing down what I was doing. Since it came to me intuitively, I was not sure if others could do it too, or if it was just my gift. By the way, I believe that all creativity comes from our sixth sense, our intuition.

To my surprise, the information I wrote seemed to be logical. I realized that I had developed HART by using my own creative tools and theories in combination with those from Gestalt, Psychosynthesis, Behaviorism, Transactional Analysis, Biofeedback, and Bioenergetics, plus some theories of Freud, Jung, Rogers, and Satir.

Then I decided to see if I could share it with others. In my very first class, I had eight eager students. A few months into the course, I returned home very excited. With a big smile on my face, I exclaimed to my partner, "It is teachable! The students are getting it!"

In fact, the students loved the process and saw how holistic, loving, and empowering it was. I was thrilled that they could also use the techniques of HART and experience successful results with their clients and themselves.

With great enthusiasm I continued to offer classes in this empowering modality. In order to reach more people, I lectured extensively, appeared numerous times in the media, and created many books, tapes, and articles explaining the concepts and tools.

I am pleased to offer you this book, which will bring HART to you in a unique way. To begin with, I will list some of the basic principles.

1. Everyone is basically good and makes the right decisions unless taught otherwise.
2. We all need love and acceptance to grow.
3. We make decisions based on our experiences. If we create new experiences, we can then make new decisions.
4. One way we learn is by modeling.
5. We all have four basic parts: physical, emotional, mental, and spiritual. We need to own and balance all four parts to be a whole person and experience inner peace.
6. There are only two basic emotions: love and fear. All other emotions are expressions of love or fear. Fear is the cause of our problems and love is the answer or solution.
7. We all have the same basic sub-personalities. Our loving ones are a nurturing parent and a free child. Our fear-based sub-personalities include a critical parent, a scared inner child, an adaptive child (people pleaser), and a rebellious child.
8. We all feel afraid sometimes, and if we don't acknowledge our fears we often become critical, rebellious (active aggressive), or adaptive (passive aggressive).
9. Anger is a secondary emotion. Under anger is always a primary feeling of fear (hurt or powerlessness).
10. We need to release our fears before we can truly accept others and ourselves.
11. We are not able to live fully in the present until we complete unfinished business from the past.

12. We all need to grow at our own pace.
13. What we do not like in ourselves, we do not like in others and visa versa.
14. Our minds are like magnets, and therefore we attract what we are thinking. (Like attracts like.)
15. We often unconsciously project on others what we are thinking and feeling.
16. Our present issues trigger our past experiences and decisions.
17. Our upsets are often "teachers" for us as they point out where we are feeling fear instead of love.
18. We all have a left and a right brain. The left side is the part of us that is logical and functional. The right side of the brain is the one that is feeling, creative and intuitive. We are all either left- or right-brain dominant.
19. To be balanced, we need to own and express both our left and right brains.
20. We take in information in different ways. They are either hearing, seeing or experiencing. (In HART we use all three ways.)
21. Addictions are what we do to the extreme in order to run away from our emotional pain caused by our negative decisions. They are usually the symptoms and not the causes of our problems.
22. No matter what our age, sex, religion, economic status, or profession is, everyone needs and deserves love, respect, appreciation, and acknowledgment.
23. What people say or do is about them and not you. You are okay no matter what people say or do!

These basic principles will be explained further in the different chapters.

Chapter 3

The Essence

The essence of HART is based on the three levels of consciousness. Freud labeled them the superego, ego, and id. I refer to them as the <u>high conscious</u>, <u>conscious</u>, and <u>subconscious</u> (or unconscious) parts of us. Everyone can access all of these states of being. It is important to be able to shift into the specific level that will enable you to act appropriately to whatever is happening.

However, a majority of people spend most of their time in their conscious level and are unaware of their subconscious and high conscious. That means that they are living life with one third of themselves. Imagine how limiting it would be to live in one third of your home. Have you been aware of your three states of consciousness?

Imagine a house that has three floors. The "attic" or top floor is where we find the high conscious. The "first floor" is symbolic of the conscious, and the "basement" represents the subconscious. To live fully and to better understand others and ourselves, it is helpful to be able to access all three floors.

High Conscious

In the "attic" we connect with the <u>high conscious</u>. This is the part of us that is creative, free, unlimited, unconditionally loving, wise, faithful, and trusting. It is also referred to as: the higher self, spirit, "Wise Person", all good and all knowing part, sixth sense, super ego, and God-Self.

When we are in this state, we are likely to experience peace, bliss, joy, love, and acceptance. There are no fears or questions here, just insights and solutions. It is not programmable. It is our all-wise, all-knowing, and all-loving state of being.

Do you recall experiencing this high level? Where were you? What were you doing? What did you do or not do that enabled you to raise yourself to that state?

Clients and students have told me that it was the same high they had experienced with drugs or alcohol. Could it be that some people take addicting, altering drugs in order to experience their higher self? How wonderful it is to know that you can get there in a natural, healthy way whenever you choose. It is always available to you, 24 hours a day, seven days a week. It is like having a 'feel good' experience with your all-wise consultant—and it's legal and free!

One way to connect with your higher self is to listen to your intuition, which is your sixth sense. I suggest that you trust your gut feelings, or what you hear or see with your inner ears and eyes, or your pure knowing, which is known as telepathy. Everyone is intuitive. It comes with the human package.

However you choose to connect with your higher self or spirit, I suggest that you set your intent to spend as much time as you can in this level. Then you will have a way to help yourself feel good, receive guidance, and act in loving ways to others and yourself.

Conscious

Now we will move on to the conscious state on the "first floor" of your home. This is the part of us that is aware of what we perceive is happening. Our logical minds and five senses (see, hear, smell, touch, and taste) are offering us information. For example, I am aware that my body is comfortable in a firm desk chair and I smell the scent of blossoms in the air.

Most people are very familiar with this mental state of being because this is where we often need to be in order to work and take care of others and ourselves. It is our human, functioning part.

The mind is like a computer in that it is programmed. In other words, it makes decisions based on experiences or data. Therefore, if you learned in school that 100 + 100 = 200, you have that memory in your mind, and you can call on it whenever you need to use that information. However, if you have learned that 100 + 100 = 250, you will think that is the truth. Therefore, the accuracy of the information in the conscious level is based on your experiences.

Subconscious

Now we will move on to the "basement". In the subconscious (also referred to as the unconscious, lower self, id, instinctive behavior) we find fears, limitations, beliefs, and cell memories. The information is based on natural instincts and decisions that are made from our experiences. Often, they are not based on reality.

An extreme example of being stuck in the subconscious can be found in the cases of the mentally ill. The people suffering from paranoia believe that others are out to get them.

I believe that most people have some unrealistic fears. For example there is the fear of flying, heights, elevators, or swimming. Or more personally, people are afraid that they are not good enough because they were often criticized as a child. Unfortunately, we project our past decisions onto others. For example, we often think and feel that our boss or partner believes that we are not good enough.

Since the subconscious level is controlled mostly by the decisions we made from our experiences, our perception of reality is unique to us. For example, you may be upset with your boss, but you don't know why. He is basically a nice person, but you feel anxious whenever he is around and you react strongly to his comments. It could be that you are relating to him as an authority figure and he reminds you of a critical parent or teacher.

In the conscious state we are usually aware of our upsets or good feelings (*symptoms*), but we are often not aware of our decisions (*causes*) that are stored in the "basement". Therefore, if we want to change our lives, we need to go to the "basement" to clear out the old, negative decisions and create new, positive ones. That is exactly what the HART processes will assist you to do.

The following is an outline of your "House":

"ATTIC"

In the ""attic"" we connect with the high conscious part of us, which is not programmable. It is also referred to as: the higher self, spirit, "Wise Person," all-good and all-knowing part, unlimited, unconditionally loving, sixth Sense, super ego, God-Self, and wisdom.

"FIRST FLOOR"

On the "first floor" we perceive everything through our conscious state, which is programmable. It is also referred to as: the mind, thoughts, communication, actions, ego, observable behavior, five senses, and awareness.

"BASEMENT"

When we are in the ""basement"", we relate to our subconscious, which is partially programmable (human instincts are not). This part is also known as: the unconscious, lower self, id, instincts, survival-based thoughts, fears, limitations, and cell memories.

To summarize, in the HART Process we go up to the "attic" (high conscious) to receive our guidance (intuitive wisdom), love, and ego-strength so that we can connect with our fears in the "basement" and overcome them. In a sense we are cleaning out our "basement". It is on the "first floor" (conscious level) where we experience the *symptoms* of our fears (the *causes*), which are found in the subconscious.

Another way I explain the HART phenomenon is with the image of an unhealthy tree. We can see the branches, which represent the negative things happening in our lives (*symptoms*).

Some examples of our conscious negative *symptoms* (branches) are: unhealthy bodies and relationships, drug and alcohol addictions, financial struggle, overweight, unfulfilling careers, loneliness, and problems with sexuality.

What we cannot see are the unhealthy underground roots of the tree filled with our negative thoughts that create our unhappiness (*causes*).

Some examples of the common unconscious *causes* of our problems (in the roots) are the negative beliefs that we are: not okay, unlovable, not good enough, unworthy, unimportant, stupid, unattractive, and a bad person.

Just like a tree that has to be healed of its problems through the roots, in the HART process we focus on changing the negative beliefs in our roots to positive ones and then our symptoms, or branches, can also be positive and healthy.

Some of our specific goals are to change our unconscious beliefs to: *I am okay, lovable, good enough, worthy, important, intelligent, attractive, and a good person.*

As a result, we will be able to enjoy high self-esteem, a healthy body, prosperity, our desired weight, fulfilling relationships and sexuality, satisfying careers, and happiness (healthy branches).

Now that you have a basic understanding of this modality, we will begin to explore ways to help you create what you want in your life through HART.

Note: If you are a counselor, the following general guidelines will also be helpful:

1. As you continue to grow, you can also help your clients heal. (For example: If you won't deal with your fears or anger, you will probably have the same problem with your clients. Your unconscious may block them from dealing with emotions that you are not comfortable addressing.)
2. Trust your intuition and feelings.
3. Trust the client's body language and tensions rather than the mind talking. The body offers accurate information; the mind may not, because it is programmable.
4. Be a model for your clients. (For example: if you want to help them to be responsible, then it is important for you to be responsible.)
5. Use your creativity and accept each client unconditionally.

Part II

Insights and Solutions
for
Successful Living

Chapter 4

Success Questionnaire

*W*ith the HART process, I have helped thousands of people actualize their goals in every area of their lives. To begin with, it is important to understand what I mean when I say success. I developed this perspective based on what I experienced in my counseling office. I had clients who were married, earned well over $100,000 a year, and were in positions of power and influence. Most people would consider them successful. But they told me that they felt frustrated, depressed, and unsuccessful. I was surprised, as you also may be.

Many of us were taught that success is an external thing—something that others give to us and is measured by accomplishments. We often say, "If only I am offered that new job, promotion, contract or raise, then I will be successful. If only that person will marry me, I will be happy." Then we actualize what we want in our career and relationship and we may be happy for a while, but it does not last. We soon feel miserable again—empty inside.

How does this happen? I have found that success is not found outside. Nobody can give it to us. My clients and my own life experiences have taught me: "Success is an internal feeling of fulfillment, peace, and power that comes from being who you are and doing what you truly want to do."

We are the only ones who can feel our joy or our pain. We are the only ones who can feel our success. That wonderful, internal, successful feeling is what I would like to help you experience in your life.

Are you ready for the fascinating journey to success? I welcome you to join me. As with many adventures, there are surprises. Be prepared for some unexpected revelations. With determination and perseverance you can overcome them and reach your destination. Setting your intent and going forward with an open mind will help you create what you want, be who you are, and experience true success.

Success Questionnaire

The following questionnaire will help you to discover the beliefs that support your success. It will also uncover possible blocks that are sabotaging your success.

I suggest that you read each statement and put a "T" for a true statement and an "F" for a false statement. It is best to write down your first response.

Life in General
____1. I deserve to be happy.
____2. I feel good when I get what I want.
____3. When I am successful, my friends will be happy for me.
____4. My parents encourage me to be more successful than them.
____5. If I am not happy at my job I leave and find another one.
____6. I appreciate it when my parents encourage me to succeed.
____7. I feel okay when I am happy, even when others are not.
____8. I notice that when things start going well, good things keep happening.
____9. I like it when people notice me.
____10. I feel comfortable with compliments.
____11. People notice me when I do well.
____12. I am intelligent.
____13. I am good enough.
____14. I am important.
____15. I am worthy.
____16. I am okay.
____17. I am attractive.
____18. When people ask me to do things, I can say "no".

___19. I believe that I can be a successful career woman and have a relationship.

___20. People accept me for who I am.

___21. I feel it is safe to be me.

Career

___1. I know what I want to do for a career.

___2. I am *not* a procrastinator.

___3. When I am successful, I believe that I will have enough time for my family and myself.

___4. I can be famous and maintain my privacy.

___5. I can be at the top and have many people in my life.

___6. Women and minorities have a chance to be successful.

___7. I can be very successful and encourage others to also be in their power.

___8. I do *not* have to hurt other people to become successful.

Money

___1. Money is *not* the root of all evil.

___2. I deserve to be prosperous.

___3. Many rich people are nice and generous.

___4. Money does *not* necessarily change people.

___5. Even though I came from a poor family, I can imagine myself with an abundance of money.

___6. Life does *not* have to be a struggle.

___7. I do *not* believe that I have to work very hard to make money.

___8. I do *not* feel guilty when I spend money.

___9. I trust myself to be responsible with money.

___10. When I have money, I will *not* necessarily have to take care of others.

___11. I can make more money than my partner and he/she feels okay.

___12. I am *not* worried about people stealing my money.

___13. I can handle the responsibility of having an abundance of money.

___14. I can be spiritual and prosperous.

Relationships

___1. I prefer dating over one-night stands.

___2. I feel good about committing to a marriage.

___3. I can handle a successful career and a relationship.
___4. I believe that there is someone out there for me.
___5. I am attractive and lovable.
___6. If I let people really get to know me, they will like me.
___7. I am being vulnerable and I am *not* afraid of getting hurt.
___8. I can handle the responsibility of a relationship.
___9. Men/women do *not* want to control me.
___10. Even though I left my last partner, I deserve to be happy.
___11. I believe that people I love stay with me.
___12. If I am in a fulfilling relationship, my friends will *not* be jealous.
___13. I believe that relationships can last.
___14. I believe that I can be in a relationship and be free to be me.
___15. I am good enough for a loving relationship.
___16. I am good person and I deserve a loving relationship.

Sex
___1. People want to be with me for who I am and *not* only for sex.
___2. I do *not* feel too vulnerable when I am sexual.
___3. I do *not* feel I have to perform for my partner.
___4. I do *not* feel pressured to have an orgasm to please my partner.
___5. I feel good about enjoying my sexuality.
___6. If I initiate sex, my partner will *not* feel I am too aggressive.
___7. If I enjoy sex, men will *not* think I am loose.
___8. If I enjoy sex, women will not think it is all I want from them.
___9. I am *not* afraid to become addicted to sex.

Weight
___1. I am successful when I try to lose weight.
___2. I can maintain my desired weight.
___3. I feel safe even when I am slim.
___4. When I started to develop, people did *not* tease me.
___5. I still feel strong when I am slim.

___6. I associate being slim with being healthy and *not* sick.
___7. When I was growing up, we had enough food for everyone in the family.
___8. My best times with my family were *not only* around the dinner table.
___9. I am choosing to lose weight, even if my partner and others nag me about it.
___10. When I am slim, I do *not* worry about dating and being rejected.
___11. When I am slim and attractive, I can resist sexual advances.
___12. If I am slim, people will *not* want me only for my body.
___13. When things start going well, I do *not* find myself overeating.
___14. I do *not* substitute food for love.

Health
___1. I have always been healthy.
___2. I do *not* get ill or hurt to get attention.
___3. When things start going well, I do *not* hurt myself or have accidents.
___4. When I am sick, I can still fulfill many of my responsibilities.
___5. I am well and I can stay home from work and relax.
___6. I deserve to feel good and to be healthy.
___7. I am independent and I take care of myself.

Sports/ Talent
___1. When I do well in sports, people do *not* think that I am dumb.
___2. I feel okay when men lose to women in sports.
___3. I can imagine myself as a winner.
___4. I am willing to do things that my parents or siblings do well.
___5. I am an artist or a musician and I am prosperous.
___6. I am doing well in sports, etc. and people like me.

How did you do? Were you surprised at some of your answers? All the statements that were <u>true</u> to you indicate beliefs you have that support your success. The opposite is true for your <u>false</u> answers. These thoughts may sabotage your success.

The goal of this chapter is to help you have all <u>true</u> answers so that you can allow yourself to succeed. You may want to repeat the questionnaire after you have read this section and have worked with the HART exercises in Part III.

Chapter 5

Seven Major Keys to Success

*I*t is interesting how I discovered the keys to success. As I was counseling my clients, I noticed that similar fears kept coming up that sabotaged them from getting what they wanted. I realized that the fears all fit into seven major categories. Then I changed the negative beliefs to positive statements and came up with the *Seven Major Keys to Success*. They are:

1. I am comfortable with the unknown.
2. Success fits my self-image.
3. I deserve success.
4. I am successful and people like me.
5. I am comfortable with what comes with success.
6. I am more successful than my parents and they love me.
7. I am successful because I choose to be.

Can you relate to these positive beliefs? Would you say, "Yes!" to each one? To have all the keys to success, it is important to overcome the corresponding fears.

Now we are ready to explore what I found to be the real causes of our frustrations, painful relationships, unfulfilling careers, financial struggles, etc. These are the *Seven Major Fears of Success*. Once we release the negative beliefs and change them to positive ones, we can actualize our goals. The following is an outline of the fears and an example of each. The

(P) refers to the positive thought and the (N) indicates the negative thought.

The Seven Major Keys to Success and the Fears to Overcome

1. (P)* I am comfortable with the unknown.
   (N) I have a fear of the unknown. Example:
   "I don't know what it would be like to be in a slim body or in a successful relationship or career."

2. (P)* Success fits my self-image.
   (N) Success does not fit my self-image. Example:
   "I wouldn't know who I was, if I were slim."

3. (P)* I deserve success.
   (N) I do not deserve success. Example:
   "I feel guilty because I once stole money from my parents."

4. (P)* I am successful and people like me.
   (N) People will not like me if I am successful. Example:
   "If I am successful in my talent or career, people won't like me."

5. (P)* I am comfortable with what comes with success.
   (N) Success has scary consequences. Example:
   "If I get the promotion I won't have enough time to spend with my family."

6. (P)* I am more successful than my parents and they love me.
   (N) My parents won't love me if I am more successful than they are. Example:
   "I don't want my father/mother to feel bad."

7. (P)* I am successful because I choose to be.
   (N) To be successful is to fulfill my parents' wishes and I am angry at them. Example:
   "I'll show them. I won't have a successful career."

Do you recognize any of these seven major fears of success? If you do, you are not alone. I found some of them to be in all of my clients. The good news is that you can overcome them and allow yourself to succeed.

It is my belief that we are all very powerful beings. If we are not accomplishing what we want in our lives, it is likely that we have an investment in not achieving our goals. We are actually unconsciously pushing away the very success we desire.

Basically we all want to feel free to fly. The image of a beautiful, rainbow colored, hot air balloon is one way I explain this phenomenon. When we take off into the air, symbolically we are free to actualize a specific goal. However, if there are seven ropes holding us down to the ground, we are stuck. As much as we want to go up, the ropes prevent us from taking off and creating what we want in our lives.

Each major rope represents one of the seven major fears of success that I have discovered. I noticed that some people were held down by all seven fears and others by only one or two. No matter how many ropes we have keeping us stuck, we need to identify the fears and release them before we can take off and actualize our goals. Until we cut free from these ropes, these fears, we continue to sabotage our success.

How do we sabotage our success? We find excuses for pushing away what we want. For example, we are offered a job and then we think about all the reasons for not taking it. We may say such things as: "I can't handle all the responsibility; I don't have enough experience; I am not smart enough; or the company is not right for me."

Or we take the job and prove these fears with our behavior. We come late, make many mistakes, procrastinate, or argue with the boss and other employees. We may even get sick, or create an accident.

We also sabotage our relationships. We meet someone very special and we start getting close. Suddenly we begin to find fault with each other. "Her nose is too big. He's too short." We become demanding and we start arguments. We make commitments and then break them.

We drive each other crazy! We say, "Come close, I want to love you and share my life with you. But stay away because I am scared. I am afraid if I am vulnerable I will get hurt." Our fears can cause us to push away the very opportunities and people we desire.

It is interesting to note that clients often came into the office telling me that they had fears of failure. In fact, no one ever complained about his or her fear of success. However, during their counseling sessions, they realized that the fear of failure was only the top of the iceberg. Underneath, deep in their unconscious, was the fear of success. Once I assisted them to uncover their fears and break through them, they allowed themselves to have what they wanted.

This concept may be as surprising to you as it was for me. I was amazed to discover that many of my clients were actually sabotaging their success—they were unconsciously afraid to have the very things that they wanted. On a conscious level, they thought that they were failures. However, on an unconscious level, they were succeeding. They were actually succeeding in not getting what they wanted.

I had never read or heard about the fear of success. Yet that is what I kept observing in my clients of all ages and with a variety of levels of education, backgrounds, and religions. One could say it is almost an "epidemic". Once I recognized the problem, I was able to develop ways to help men, women, and children overcome their fears and achieve their goals.

I actually discovered the fear of success with my very first client. Betty told me that she felt like a failure in her relationships. "If only the right man would ask me to marry him!" said Betty. But she never seemed to be able to attract that right man.

I sensed that the answer to her problem was in her unconscious. I have a favorite saying, "Close your eyes and see clearly." So I said, "Betty, close your eyes and imagine that the right man is asking you to marry him. How do you feel?" Betty replied, "Terrified!" There it was—the first of many of my clues of the insidious fear of success.

On the conscious level Betty wanted to be loved and married. But underneath those feelings, in the unconscious level, she was afraid of it—afraid of having the relationship she desired.

As I continued to counsel, I was fascinated to discover how many men, women, and children had fears of success. My clients also taught me that even our illnesses and accidents are often caused by a fear of success. One pretty young woman discovered why she had a car accident. She felt guilty about having so much when her friends and family were struggling. The accident left her with a scar on her beautiful forehead.

When I helped people communicate with their unconscious the same negative message kept coming up—I am afraid to succeed!

Do any of these examples sound familiar? Do you recognize them in others or even yourself? The good news is that it is reversible. I will help you find the keys to your success.

In order to overcome the fears that prevent our success, we need to explore where these self-defeating beliefs come from. It is helpful to understand that there are two parts of us in our unconscious that are fighting each other. One part of us knows exactly what it wants and goes after it. I call this sub-personality the Inner Free Child. But the other part, called the Inner Scared Child, is afraid to have what the Inner Free Child wants, so it sabotages many of its efforts. This is an example of what I call the Fear of Success. We can actualize what we want in our lives, when we uncover and release these negative beliefs.

Where do there fears come from? I believe that we are all born basically healthy and positive. However, as young children we think that the world revolves around us. We take responsibility for whatever happens and we make decisions from our experiences. We are like mathematicians constantly making equations. Some examples are:

Daddy never plays with me = I am unimportant.

Mommy always criticizes me = I am bad.

Mom and Dad are fighting = I am responsible for their problem, so I must be a bad person.

My Dad left us = I am unlovable.

My teachers do not listen to me = I am worthless.

Other kids tease me = I am not good enough.

My siblings do not want to play with me = I am not okay.

There are endless examples of the many equations we make from our experiences. None of these conclusions are true. But since they are in our unconscious we believe them, and we act on them as if they are true

Our decisions make up our "life script" or "computer program." They are either positive or negative thoughts that run our lives. Our beliefs are magnetic and they draw to us whatever we are thinking.

For example, a man or women brought up in a family that was wealthy probably has the belief that there is an abundance of money. However, a person who experienced poverty, as he or she was growing up, is likely to make a decision that money is scarce. With that negative belief in his mind, he is inclined to unconsciously create his reality of not having enough money.

As we continue to grow up, we attract negative experiences into our lives to reinforce our negative decisions. In fact, if someone tells us that we are okay, we are likely to push them away, because our perception of ourselves it that we are not okay.

The basic principle of HART is that we make decisions based on our experiences. Therefore, it is first necessary to uncover the *cause* of our problem—the negative decision based on a negative experience. Then we can imagine that we are deleting, erasing or "burning away" (with a laser beam) that negative scene and change it to a positive one. From this new experience, we can make a new positive decision that supports us in creating what we want. Our positive images and thoughts draw to us what we desire.

I found that I do not have to help people to become successful. All I need to do is to help them to be aware of and overcome their unconscious fears. Then they can effortlessly allow themselves to fulfill their dreams.

Once the men and women removed the fears that were keeping them stuck, they suddenly met their perfect mate, or were offered the job or promotion they were seeking. For the first time in their lives they found losing weight to be effortless. The clients' were healing their bodies and allowing themselves to receive the money they need. They let go of their addictions and took control of their lives.

I will discuss each fear of success in detail to help you recognize these unconscious negative thoughts. Then you can work with the exercises in Part III to help you overcome any of your blocks to success.

I often say, "We are unique, but our problems are not." See if you identify with any of the clients' fears. You are on your way to experience the exhilaration of flying free in your air balloon.

1. Fear of the Unknown

For some reason, we are often afraid of the unknown. We will stay in an unfulfilling job or relationship, because we know what it is like. It is familiar. We do not know what will happen if we make a change. One client once said, "I would rather be safe than satisfied." Can you relate to that?

An example of this fear of success is the story of Bill, a forty-two year old parole officer. He complained that he was burned-out and wanted to quit his job. However, Bill was afraid to leave it for something he really wanted to do.

I asked Bill to close his eyes and to see an image of himself many years from now still working at the job he was afraid to leave. Bill visualized an unhappy and very tired-looking man. I then asked Bill what he wanted to say to that image of his future self. Bill replied, "I wish you had the courage to leave that job and do what you really wanted."

Then I asked Bill what he wanted to do now. He responded, "I want to leave my job and pursue another career, and I am going to do just that!" "Even though you are scared?" I asked. "Yes," Bill said with a calm and certain voice, "Even though I am scared."

I continued to guide Bill to imagine himself in the future doing what he loved. He visualized himself in his new career looking happy and fulfilled. Bill then had the courage to leave his job and follow his heart.

Often we need to be in a lot of pain before we are willing to move on. Sometimes the death of a loved one, a divorce, a birthday, or a severe illness awakens us so that we can see clearly—become aware of our true desires.

I woke up on my 30th birthday and realized how unhappy I was with my life. I said to myself, "Helene, you have suffered enough. You are not going to spend the next thirty years like the last thirty." That was when I began to grow, take risks and create what I wanted in my life. That was when I made a commitment to be me, to be happy, and to feel good.

I cannot make that commitment for you. I am not that powerful and no one else is either. Only *you* can make that decision.

In order to have what you want in your life, I suggest that you say to yourself, "I am tired of being in pain and suffering. I do not want to settle anymore. I am ready to move on, even though I am scared of the unknown. Success and happiness are what I really want." When you make that commitment to yourself, you are likely to start noticing positive changes in your life.

2. Success Does Not Fit My Self-image

I discovered that we all unconsciously have an image of ourselves. If our image is not in alignment with our desired goal, then we are likely to sabotage it.

If your image of yourself is that of an employee, you are not likely to allow yourself to become a manager. It just does not fit your self-image.

If you see yourself as unlovable, you will probably push away the one who tells you, "You are lovable." If you have an image of yourself as being poor, you very well may sabotage your financial success and any chance to move up in your career.

For example, I wanted to join an exclusive tennis club in California and I heard myself sabotaging my enrollment by thinking negative thoughts. *I do not have enough money. I cannot play tennis well. I have no time. People will not want to play with me.* Since none of these statements were true, I recognized my fear of success. Being a member of the exclusive tennis club did not fit my self-image, which was a poor girl from Brooklyn, New York.

My unconscious fears could not accept a poor-girl image in this club with wealthy people. Once I realized the issue, I was able to use the HART process to update my self-image. I did allow myself to join the tennis club and I had a wonderful time. I broke through the fear that being a member did not fit my self-image.

How many clubs or organizations have you not joined because it did not fit your self-image?

This fear of success comes up very often in love relationships. Susan, a twenty-six year old attractive blonde, was in tears as she told me how much she wanted to be in a relationship. However, all the men in her life kept leaving her.

In order for Susan to feel lovable, I guided her through a process that helped her change her self-image. It was not long before she began to attract more successful relationships.

Do you have a successful self-image? If not, it is time to release the old image and replace it with one that is in alignment with your goals.

3. I Do Not Deserve Success

I learned from my clients that most of us are blocking our health, happiness, and/or success because we do not believe we deserve it. I also discovered that we are all basically good, because clients who were not even caught doing something wrong still felt guilty and punished themselves by sabotaging their success.

An example of this is Joan, a fifty-year-old woman, who made a lot of money and then lost it all. I asked her to close her eyes and say, "I can't be successful, because ____," and finish the sentence. Joan replied, "I can't be successful, because I am bad." I then said, "Go back to the time you decided that you were bad." Joan saw herself stealing money out of her parents' cash register when she was ten years old. No one caught her, but she felt guilty and she was still punishing herself forty years later.

I then asked Joan to imagine that her parents were there in the store and to speak to them. She said, "Mom and Dad, I am really sorry. Please forgive me." Then Joan imagined that they were forgiving her and she forgave herself. At that point, she sighed with relief and said, "Wow! I have been carrying that around for a long time."

We can feel guilty about anything no matter how long ago it happened. It is important to become aware of whatever we believe was wrong. Then we can stop punishing ourselves by letting it go with forgiveness.

Another example of this fear of success is the case of a seventeen-year-old athlete. Rick was doing very well in sports until he fell and severely hurt his knee. Rick realized that when his parents spanked him as a young child he had decided that he must be a bad person. Therefore, Rick concluded that he did not deserve to be successful.

I have found that men or women, who leave a relationship or other commitment, very often feel guilty. Jim, a thirty-six-year-old man, had left his wife and children two years ago. He was still feeling depressed and unhappy in his work and new relationship.

To assist Jim, I asked him to close his eyes and imagine that he was a judge in a courtroom. He was looking at an image of himself as the prisoner who was up for parole. I said, "Judge Jim, tell the prisoner Jim what he did wrong and what his sentence should be." Judge Jim replied, "You are a terrible person. You left your wife and children. I am sentencing you to a lifetime of misery!"

I continued, "Okay, Judge Jim. Send him back to prison for life." But then he answered, "No! He needs three more years of pain." "All right," I said. "No", replied Judge Jim. "Today is prisoner Jim's birthday. He has suffered enough. Prisoner Jim, you are free to go and be happy," expressed Judge Jim.

This empowering HART process helped Jim let go of his guilt, leave his self-made prison, and go on with his life. That is what we all need to do. Only then can we believe that we deserve success and happiness.

Do you have an internal judge (critical parent) punishing you for things you feel you did wrong?

4. People Will Not Like Me If I Am Successful

Many of us have experienced rejection when we were growing up. Other kids, siblings, friends, relatives, and even parents may have been jealous of our good looks, intelligence, talents, and achievements. Therefore, we are afraid that people will not like us if we succeed. We may sabotage ourselves in order to be accepted and loved.

One of my clients discovered during her counseling session that she was often sick in elementary school because she was very bright and the kids rejected her. By missing many classes, Mary's grades dropped and she was more accepted by her peers. Mary was shocked when she realized that she was still following the same pattern in her adult life. She then understood why she was not allowing herself to be healthy, or successful in her career.

We can also have adult fears of being all that we are. One common example is Sandy's story. She was a forty-two-year-old single parent who felt she was a failure in her commercial real estate job. Sandy was not making enough money to support her three children.

I said, "Sandy, close your eyes and visualize yourself doing well and earning the amount of money you want. How are you feeling?" Sandy replied, "Scared!" When I asked her what she was afraid of, Sandy replied, "I am afraid if I make a lot of money, no man will want me."

I then asked Sandy if she was willing to believe that she could have the career, the money, and the relationship she wanted. She said, "Yes." Since visualization is very powerful, I suggested that she see herself financially abundant and in a loving relationship.

A month later, Sandy called me and said, "Helene, I think you had better sit down. I earned $40,000 this month!"

That is how quickly this process can work. It is not magic, although it proves how powerful we are to create what we want. Sandy was unconsciously pushing away financial success, because she was afraid that men would not like her. When she released that fear, she allowed prosperity into her life.

The fear that people will not like you if you are successful can stop you in any area of your life. I often hear people say, "My sibling will reject me if I do too well." "My husband will feel threatened if I earn too much money." "People will not play with me if I am too good." "Other employees will resent me if I get a promotion." "My best friend will be upset if I am thinner than her." "My friends will be jealous if I am in a relationship."

We often unconsciously hold ourselves back and stop ourselves from reaching our true potential and being happy, because we are afraid of being rejected and being alone. What is important to realize is that our relationships have problems when we do not feel free to fulfill ourselves. That is, we often feel resentful and angry when we hold ourselves back. These negative feelings hurt our relationships.

When we allow ourselves to actualize what we want in our lives, we attract people who accept and support our happiness. Also, when we are successful, we provide a healthy model for others who really want to reach their own potential. Therefore, being successful is a gift to them and to you.

5. Success Has a Scary Consequence

I often hear people tell me, "Yes. I want to be successful, but I do not want all the worry and responsibility that comes with it." Or they say, "If I am successful, I will not have enough free time for myself or my family." In the relationship area, the words are often, "I want a relationship, but I am afraid that I will be hurt." These are negative beliefs that we have attached to success. They need not be attached, but as long as we believe that they are, we will avoid success.

For example, I often used to sing one of the songs from the musical *Porgy and Bess*: "I've got plenty of nothing and nothing to worry about." And I was wondering why I was not creating an abundance of money in my life.

I believed that rich people had to spend a lot of time worrying about how they were going to protect themselves and their wealth. I also thought that money made people mean and greedy. I certainly did not want to be mean or greedy, or worry about personal safety and my things. Therefore, my unconscious fears kept pushing away the prosperity I worked for and desired.

Once I become aware of my negative beliefs associated with money, I replaced them with positive thoughts. I believed that I could have money and feel happy, relaxed, and safe, and be a kind and generous person. Then I allowed an abundance of money into my life.

At a very early age, we begin attaching fears and negative beliefs to our image of success. I worked with teen-agers who were doing poorly in school and behaving irresponsibly at home. I asked, "Do you want to grow up?" They often replied, "No. Grown-ups never have any fun. All they do is work, worry, and pay bills."

To assist them, I ask them to visualize themselves as adults handling their responsibilities and having fun. Once they let go of their fear that growing up necessarily means all work and no play, the improvement in their behavior at home and in their school performance was remarkable.

The way I see it, success is like a delicious, red apple that we want very much to eat. But we don't dare take a bite out of the apple if we imagine that there is a green worm in it—that is the scary consequence. We first have to remove the worm from the apple, let go of the associated fear, so that we can take a bite of success.

An example of this phenomenon is Fred's story. He was sabotaging his business, because he was unconsciously afraid that if he were successful he would not have enough time to spend with his children. That was the "worm" he was trying to avoid.

I guided Fred back to the time when he made that decision and he saw himself as a young boy. His father was very successful in his business and he rarely spent time with his children. I helped Fred realize that he was not his father and that he could be both successful in business and have time to spend with his children. He could have the apple without the "worm."

Another example is John, a fifty-two-year-old successful manager, who wanted to become president of his company. When I asked him to close his eyes and imagine that he was in that position, he felt scared. John realized that unconsciously he was afraid of the responsibility that comes with that role. The part of John that was afraid was sabotaging him from moving on in his career.

In another case, Bob, a twenty-eight year old engineer, was angry with his boss for not delegating more responsibility to him. Under all that anger was fear—he was afraid he was not smart enough to do the job.

I asked Bob to go back to the time when he made the decision that he was dumb. Bob recalled an incident when he was four years old. He needed his grandfather's assistance to tie his shoes. The little boy felt he had to act stupid in order to gain the extra attention. The decision Bob had made, "If I'm intelligent, I won't get attention," followed him into adult life. Bob recognized his fear of success and made a new decision, "I am intelligent and I get enough attention." At the next counseling session Bob smiled as he told me how his boss was giving him more responsibility.

I am convinced that one reason we struggle financially is because of our issues around money. I have discovered twenty fears of success that block us from prosperity. (Note Part III)

For example, Dave told me that even though he worked hard and tried to earn an abundance of money, he just was not making it. In his counseling session, Dave regressed back to the time when he was ten years old and in church with his parents. He vividly saw the priest standing at the pulpit with his hand raised in condemnation as he said, "Rich people are evil!" At that point Dave decided that if he were rich, he would be evil.

When Dave realized that money is only a piece of paper, an energy exchange, and that he could be rich and a good person, he began to accumulate the wealth he deserved and desired.

I have had numerous male clients who were sabotaging their relationships because of their issues with money. They were concerned about taking on the responsibility of the financial commitment that a marriage may entail. The men were relieved when they discovered that they were okay even if their wife helped with their finances and even if their wives earned more money than they did.

This fear of scary consequences explains why many men and women avoid relationships or marriage. Sometimes they are afraid they will not have enough time for their business or profession, or free time for themselves. Once they believe that they can have it all, they allow themselves the intimacy and companionship they desire.

One of the scariest consequences that men and women connect with relationships is the fear of being hurt. One part of them wants a relationship and the other unconsciously pushes it away. To help them deal with their rejections or frustrations about not finding anyone to love, I ask them to close their eyes and visualize their hearts. They often see their hearts shrunken, bruised, stabbed with knives, or even encased in iron. They vividly see that they are carrying emotional wounds from the past.

When I ask the clients to see if they built a wall around themselves for protection, they often visualize a thick, high wall made of bricks, concrete or stone. I then ask them how they feel behind their walls. Their response is usually, "I feel safe but lonely". After I guide them back to the times their hearts were hurt, and they burn away the painful scenes and create a positive one, they feel better.

In fact, their self-esteem increases and they actually visualize their wall crumbling and their hearts healed. They feel stronger and okay about themselves. I share with them that they are okay, no matter what anyone says, does or thinks. Then if someone chooses not to be with them, they do not feel devastated. Instead they move on to meet people who are open to them.

I have found that only after their heart looked healed and healthy were they ready to allow people to get close to them and allow themselves to be in intimate relationships. They successfully removed the fear that a relationship means hurt and pain.

The fear that success is associated with getting hurt is also very common in people who are overweight. I often hear about their pattern of going on diets and losing weight, but their success is temporary. They soon gain all the weight back—and some more.

I recall Terry, a 35-year-old woman, who was fifty pounds overweight and never succeeded in any of the diet programs she attempted. When we explored her weight issue, we found out that she actually felt safe behind her wall of fat. When Terry was slim she was very attractive, and she received a lot of unwanted looks and attention from men. When she was overweight they left her alone. Terry began to understand why each time she came close to her desired weight, she lost control and quickly regained all the weight she had lost.

I helped Terry feel confident that she could handle the attention in a positive way. Then she felt that she could be thin, attractive, and safe. Terry can have the success she desires without the scary consequence.

I have uncovered fifteen fears of success about being slim. (Note Part III) To get in touch with the cause of the client's problem, I often say, "Close your eyes and visualize yourself at your desired weight." Then I say, "How do you feel?" They are often very surprised when they realize that they feel weak, small, and vulnerable. They are afraid if they succeed in losing weight, they will not be safe.

An example of this is Eve, a forty-two-year-old woman with a serious weight problem. When Eve was young and slim, men would pick her up and toss her into the air. She felt totally powerless. Eve vowed to herself that no man would ever be able to mistreat her that way again. At her present weight, she is getting what she wants; no man can lift her. The truth is that Eve can be slim and powerful. She can have the apple without the worm.

Are you aware of any scary consequences you have associated with success? If you are, then you can release them and take a bite out of the big, delicious apple of success.

6. My Parents Won't Love Me If I Am More Successful Than They Are

I was surprised to discover that many clients were unconsciously afraid that if they were successful their mom and/or dad would not love them. This issue came up even though sometimes their parents had been deceased for many years. Our fears, like all of our emotions, can be irrational. However, they are still very real to us and definitely affect our lives.

The life situation of a fifty-two-year-old man demonstrates this major fear of success. Dennis was destroying his third marriage. Every time he married a woman he loved and was happy, he began to sabotage his life. He would start arguments with his wife, mess up at work and drink heavily.

Dennis's mother had been very unhappy in her life and that included an unfulfilling marriage. Being her first born, he unconsciously felt guilty about leaving her and being happy himself. His mother's words were, "When you leave home and get married, I will no longer be part of your life." Dennis realized that he was finding ways to destroy his success and happiness so that his mother would continue to love him.

After he overcame this fear and some other fears of success, Dennis was able to allow himself to be happy in his marriage and his career.

This fear has also showed up with women who sabotaged their careers, because they did not want their fathers to feel bad. Some women said, "If I make more money than my father, he won't love me anymore."

In this modern age, we have the potential of living longer, earning more money, and being healthier, happier, and more successful in our relationships. Whether our parents are alive or deceased, we can still have an image in our unconscious of them—of their words and their pain.

To resolve this issue, I ask my clients to close their eyes and imagine that their parents are standing in front of them. I suggest that they ask their mother and father, "Will you still love me if I am happier and more successful than you are (or were)?" The clients often see their parents smile and hear them encouraging them to be as happy and as successful as they can be.

However, if either one or both parents respond in a negative way, then I suggest to the man or woman that he or she express compassion for the parent's pain and forgive him or her.

Then I guide the client to create a new image of nurturing parents who will support them in getting what they want and in being successful. From this healing experience the clients make a new decision: "I am successful and my parents love me." Then they act out their new belief and allow themselves to be all that they are.

Do you feel your parents will love you if you are more successful than they are or were?

7. To Be Successful Is To Fulfill My Parent's Wishes and I Am Angry at Them

This last major fear of success is saying, "If I am successful, then I will be achieving my parents' ambitions and dictates over me. I am angry with my parents and I refuse to give them that satisfaction. To get back at them, I will be a failure."

It is helpful to understand more about anger. As I indicated before, in my opinion there are only two basic emotions — love and fear. All other emotions basically stem from these two. For example, kindness, caring, and compassionate feelings are all based on love. Anger, resentment, and jealousy are signs of fear. Therefore, anger is a secondary emotion. Under anger is always fear, hurt or powerlessness. When we are angry we are covering up a fear. When we are angry with others and do things out of rebellion, we often hurt ourselves.

I recall Tom, a fifty-year-old man, who shared with me that his mother had wanted him to become a lawyer. Tom went to law school, but then dropped out. Then she wanted him to become a doctor. An obedient son, Tom enrolled in Medical School, but he dropped out of that too. Tom then was hired for many different jobs—none of which he liked. In fact, he felt like a failure.

I asked Tom to close his eyes and to imagine himself as a little boy looking up at his mother. "What do you want to say to her, Tom? There are no consequences, because she is not here," I said.

Tom responded, "Mom, I am furious at you. All you did was yell at me and punish me. Stop being so mean! Either you scream at me or ignore me. You never have anything nice to say. I could never please you. I'll show you. I won't be successful like you want me to be." Tom was surprised at his response. He was not consciously aware of all the anger he was still feeling from his childhood experiences.

The tragedy was that for all these years, even though Tom's mother was deceased, he was still rebelling by sabotaging his career. Once he released his anger constructively and was able to forgive his mother, he felt love for her.

(I have found that I never have to help someone love another. I just need to help them release the anger and hurt that is blocking their loving feelings.)

I encouraged Tom to be successful, because that is what he wanted to be, and not to please or hurt anyone else. Tom was so excited about his own growth that he decided to become a therapist. For the first time in his life, he was enjoying his work. Tom overcame his fears of success. Needless to say, his wife was also very happy.

Now you have read about the Seven Major Fears of Success. Do you relate to any of them? The exact form each fear takes may vary. However, can you see how they may be stopping you from getting what you want in your life?

The good news is that you can now use the exercises and affirmations in Part III to help you overcome your fears and be all that you choose to be.

Breaking through fears of success is a continuous rewarding process, because successful people are usually moving onward and upward. You will probably find that the process gets easier. If you continue to release any fears that are causing you to sabotage yourself, you can move faster up the ladder of success and happiness,

If you are ready to have what you desire, then close your eyes and imagine that you are in your beautiful, rainbow-colored air balloon. Feel the weight (of the ropes) of the fears of success dropping off easily, so that you can take off. Look below and notice the beautiful, green meadow, the majestic mountains in the distance, and the peaceful blue sky filled with puffy white clouds. Notice that you are free to fly!

Chapter 6

Self-Esteem

Self-esteem is a measure of our self-confidence and self-respect. It also indicates how much we love and accept ourselves. To monitor the clients' progress, I ask them at the beginning and end of the session to close their eyes and to rate their self-esteem by visualizing, or sensing a number from 1-10 (10 being high). After replacing their negative thoughts with positive ones, their numbers are higher—an indication that they had succeeded in loving themselves more, in raising their self-esteem.

The clients and I were pleased and amazed at how quickly their lives showed signs of progress. Their health and relationships improved, new opportunities opened up in their careers and they felt stronger, happier, and more peacefully powerful. A higher level of self-esteem enabled them to take control of their lives and to help others to do the same.

What causes us to have low opinions of ourselves? Where do these self-defeating thoughts come from? As I expressed earlier, negative experiences are the *causes* of our negative decisions, and of course, the opposite is also true. As we are growing up and learning about others, the world and ourselves, we make decisions based on our experiences with parents, guardians, grandparents, siblings, other relatives, teachers, friends, etc.

However, because we spend most of our time with our parents or guardians, they usually have the most influence on our self-esteem. Therefore we will begin to heal the sub-personality that has our negative thoughts, called the inner scared child, by hearing the words of nurturing parents.

The following letter can assist you to love yourself. You may want to rate your self-esteem from 1-10 before and after you read it.

A Letter from a Nurturing Parent

Imagine that you have received this nurturing letter from your mother, father, grandparent, or guardian. Allow the loving, healing words to speak to the inner scared child.

My dear child, please allow me to be there for you as your nurturing parent. I want to express the part of me that I didn't know how to show you before. I really do love you. I know that in the past I wasn't always kind and loving to you. I want you to understand that because of my own problems, I sometimes acted in negative ways. What I said or did was a reflection of me and not of you. At the time I was unconsciously acting out my frustrations, or automatically doing to you what was done to me as a child. I learned how to parent from my parents, as they did with theirs, and so on down through the generations. Please forgive me for anything I did that hurt you. I never meant to do you any harm. I love you.

You are the child I wanted. You are a beautiful gift to me. You deserve to be loved and nurtured. You are a good person. You are important, worthwhile, and good enough. You are clever, creative, and talented. I marvel at your curiosity, your ability to learn, and all the wonderful things you can do. I do care about you. You are so special to me. I want you to trust that my loving part will always be here to speak to you, hold you, guide you, and love you.

My dear loving child, I want you to know that you can be more successful, happier, and healthier than I was. You have all my blessings. I will continue to love and support you in all the successes that you so much deserve. I want to encourage you to be successful because you want to be and not for me. You don't have to prove anything to me or anyone else.

I love you unconditionally and so do others. It is your life. Take control of it. Sit in the driver's seat. Go where you want to go. Do whatever you want to do. You are a unique individual. Find out who you are and be the best you can be. It is your birthright to be yourself, to be happy, and to be successful. You deserve the best of everything. I want you to feel peacefully powerful, which comes from being who you are and doing what you really want to do.

I encourage you to balance your life. It is important for you to play, have fun, enjoy yourself, take vacations, and have a good time. You will still be productive ~ even more so because play is re-energizing. Make things fun. Even make your work fun and enjoyable. Let go of the idea that it has to be difficult or a struggle, and realize that it can be easy and effortless.

One of the biggest gifts you can give to yourself is to stop what you are doing, be quiet, and ask yourself, "What do I want to do now?" Learn from the past, set your goals for the future, and live in the present. There is no anxiety when you focus totally in the present moment.

My dear child, it is important to feel all of your feelings and to express them in constructive ways. It is okay to be angry. Take responsibility for your anger and release it by yelling and hitting a soft pillow. Then ask yourself, "What am I afraid of?" Because under anger is fear. Have the courage to share your feelings with someone you trust. Once you overcome your fears, you will find that you won't be angry and hurt others or yourself.

I have total faith that you are very capable of taking care of yourself. Trust yourself to make the right decisions and to know who to trust.

Realize the truth that you can take responsibility for your life and still have fun. Please remember that people are responsible for themselves. Allowing them to do that is a gift to them and to you. You are only responsible for your thoughts, feelings, and behavior.

Accept that there is abundance in this world. Relax and let go of your belief in scarcity. There is an abundance of love, money, food, and whatever you want and need.

Know that it is safe for you to have what you want and to be who you are. Accept that people are there to support and care about you. Take risks so that you can be satisfied with your life. Have a healthy, happy, and successful self-image and that is who you will be.

My dear child, let go of any guilt feelings you have. Forgive yourself for anything you have done in the past. Remember that you did your best at the time. If you could have acted differently, you would have. Accept yourself and learn from your mistakes. If you are punishing yourself by sabotaging your happiness and success, give yourself the gift of forgiveness. Know that others and I forgive you and accept you unconditionally.

Also, my child, forgive others for their negative behavior. Remember the same applies to them. They did their best at the time. They were acting out of their hurt or fear, just as you were when you were unkind. Holding onto grudges and being angry with others really hurts you. So please give yourself the gift of forgiving others.

My dearest child, you have everything inside of you to make you happy. Love and accept yourself unconditionally ~ that is the key to happiness. You are wonderful, beautiful, and fantastic. I love you with all my heart.

Please release any hurt, resentments or anger you have towards me. Then forgive me, open up your heart, and accept my love. When you allow yourself to feel and express your love to me and love yourself unconditionally, you will grow, heal, be more positive, and create a wonderful life. You will experience loving relationships, a successful career, excellent physical health, and happiness. And you, my dear child, deserve it all.

Nurturing Your Inner Child

To further increase your self-esteem, we will now call on the sub-personality that is all-loving and accepting—the inner nurturing parent.

Imagine that you are holding your inner scared child's hand and walking on a beautiful beach. The sun is shining in the clear blue sky. You notice some birds walking on the warm sand

and others flying over the calm, green waves. Your scared child is beginning to trust that you are really there for nurturing and support and is ready to hear you. Read quietly or out loud these reassuring words—these affirmations (positive thoughts)—to your inner child.

My dear child,

1. It is okay to feel scared. Welcome to the human race.
2. You are important.
3. You are good enough.
4. You are worthy.
5. You are okay.
6. You are lovable.
7. You are attractive.
8. You are intelligent.
9. You are creative and intuitive.
10. You are competent and talented.
11. You are a good person.
12. You are wanted and you do belong.
13. You trust yourself to know whom to trust.
14. You trust your decisions.
15. You are accepting all your feelings and expressing them in healthy ways.
16. You are releasing your anger into a pillow and you and others are safe.
17. You are forgiving yourself for all your mistakes.
18. You are forgiving others for all of their negative behavior.
19. You can say "no" and you are okay.
20. You are capable of taking care of yourself.
21. You are taking control of your life and seeing your choices.
22. You are taking responsibility for your happiness.
23. You are communicating clearly what you want and need.
24. You are listening to what others want and need and creating win-win solutions.
25. You have the courage to take risks and face the unknown, even if you feel scared.
26. You are seeing yourself with an abundance of love and prosperity.
27. Your image of yourself is attractive, healthy, and happy.

28. You are slim and in control of what you eat and drink.
29. You are visualizing yourself in your successful career.
30. You are successful and people are very happy for you.
31. You are modeling success for many others and you are loved and safe.
32. You are successful in your career and in your relationships.
33. You are more successful than your parents and they love you.
34. You are successful, because *you* want to be.
35. You are prosperous and you are a good, honest, caring person.
36. You have an abundance of money and people want to be with you because they like *you*.
37. You are successful and you have enough time for yourself and loved ones.
38. You are in a loving relationship and you are free to be you.
39. You are in a lasting, fulfilling relationship and you are sharing the responsibilities with your partner.
40. You have an abundance of supportive, caring people in your life.
41. You are taking time to relax and play and you are productive.
42. You are doing things effortlessly.
43. You are taking care of yourself and you are there for others.
44. You are taking total responsibility for your life and having fun.
45. You are only responsible for your thoughts, feelings, and behavior.
46. You like yourself.
47. You love yourself.
48. You are feeling peacefully powerful.
49. You are creating what you want in your life.
50. You deserve it all!

Inner Child Affirmations

To raise your self-esteem even higher, imagine that the inner child is speaking to your adult part. Insert your name, and read, say, or sing the affirmations (note the chapter on affirmations in Part III) until these truths become a part of your automatic thinking. For example: "I, Mary, am okay."

If the positive thought does not feel right, then add the words, "beginning to believe." For example, the affirmation, "I, John, am okay" becomes, "I, John, am beginning to believe that I am okay."

1. I, <u>your name,</u>, am okay even when I am scared.
2. I, _____, am a worthwhile person.
3. I, _____ , am important.
4. I, _____, am good enough.
5. I, _____, am okay.
6. I, _____, am lovable.
7. I, _____, am attractive.
8. I, _____, am intelligent.
9. I, _____, am creative and intuitive.
10. I, _____, am competent and talented.
11. I, _____, am a good person.
12. I, _____, am wanted and I belong.
13. I, _____, trust my decisions.
14. I, _____, accept all my feelings.
15. I, _____, am expressing my feelings in healthy ways.
16. I, _____, am releasing my anger into a pillow and others and I are safe.
17. I, _____, forgive myself for all my mistakes.
18. I, _____, am forgiving others for all their mistakes.
19. I, _____, am saying "no" and I am okay.
20. I, _____, am self-caring and I am there for others.
21. I, _____, am capable of taking care of myself.
22. I, _____, am taking control of my life and seeing all of my choices.
23. I, _____, am taking responsibility for my happiness.
24. I, _____, am communicating honestly and clearly what I want and need.
25. I, _____, am listening to what others want and creating win-win solutions.

26. I, _____, am courageously facing the unknown, even though I am scared.
27. I, _____, am allowing myself an abundance of love and prosperity.
28. I, _____, see myself attractive, happy, and healthy.
29. I, _____, am slim and in control of what I eat and drink.
30. I, _____, am visualizing myself in a successful career.
31. I, _____, am successful and people are very happy for me.
32. I, _____, am modeling success for many people and I'm loved and safe.
33. I, _____, am successful in my career and in my relationships.
34. I, _____, am more successful than my parents and they love me.
35. I, _____, am successful, because I want to be.
36. I, _____, am prosperous and I am a good, honest person.
37. I, _____, have an abundance of money and people want to be with me because they like me.
38. I, _____, am successful and I have enough time for my   loved ones and myself.
39. I, _____, am allowing others to support and care about me.
40. I, _____, am in a loving relationship and I am free to be me.
41. I, _____, am in a lasting, fulfilling relationship.
42. I, _____, am taking time to relax and play and I am productive.
43. I, _____, am doing things effortlessly.
44. I, _____, am taking total responsibility for my life and I am having fun.
45. I, _____, am only responsible for my thoughts, feelings, and behavior.
46. I, _____, like myself.
47. I, _____, love myself.
48. I, _____, feel peacefully powerful.

49. I, _____, am creating what I want in my life.
50. I, _____, believe that I deserve it all.

You sure do!

The following is a summary of some of the most common core decisions that affect our self-esteem.

The Truth Is

No matter what anyone says or does, I am okay, worthy, lovable, attractive, important, intelligent, and good enough. I am a good person and I deserve to be happy, healthy, and successful!

You may now want to close your eyes and rate your self-esteem again from 1-10. How did you do? Is it a higher number?

If you find yourself unable to accept all these loving words, you may need to first release feelings of fear, hurt, or anger that are in the way. I suggest that you work with the HART self-esteem exercises in Part III.

However you choose to release your blocks to love, realize that it is probably the most important thing you will ever do. Focus on healing the inner scared child, on loving and accepting yourself—the key to health, happiness, and success. Raise your self-esteem and you will live a much happier, healthier and more successful life.

Chapter 7

Healing Your Body

Sunny, a young man in his late twenties, was diabetic from the time he was twelve years old. A former client referred him to me years ago. But he was ready to face his issues only after he began to go into diabetic shock almost daily.

In order to help Sunny heal himself, I said, "Close your eyes and imagine that you are really small and traveling inside your body to the place where you store all your tension." It was no surprise to me when Sunny ended up in front of his pancreas and said, "My God, what a mess. There's a lot of junk in there."

Then I continued, "Sunny, be aware of one of the issues you have that is stored in your pancreas." He replied, "I'm feeling terrible because my parents are always arguing." When I asked him what decision he was making from that experience he replied, "I must be responsible. I must be bad."

With the HART process, I helped Sunny release that negative belief, realize the truth that he is only responsible for himself, and that he is a good person. After the emotional healing took place, I guided Sunny back to his pancreas and he reported seeing it looking better—some "stuff" had definitely been removed.

In the course of his counseling sessions, Sunny continued to become aware of and overcome all the negative issues that were emotionally stored in his pancreas. He smiled as he told me how he was progressively feeling better.

By the eighth and final session, Sunny reported that his pancreas looked very healthy. He said, "It's amazing, Helene, I am taking less than one half of the amount of insulin I needed when I first came to see you. I realize that I almost killed myself by way of diabetic shock because I couldn't cope with all the emotional pain with my family and a broken relationship."

If Sunny had died from diabetic shock, I would have called that "legal suicide", because he was unconsciously creating his death. Obviously, Sunny also had a part of him that wanted to live. It is that positive part that finally convinced him to face his issues and heal himself.

Another example of the connection between the mind, the emotions, and the body is Cindy, a single woman in her middle thirties, who had constant vaginal yeast infections. Cindy had no relief, no matter how much she treated the condition with the medication from her doctor. During her counseling session, I guided Cindy to imagine that she was very small and traveling inside her vagina. When I asked her what she was seeing, she said, "I see lots of redness and white blotches."

I asked Cindy to imagine that she was the image of the vagina and to see herself standing in front of her. Then I said, "Vagina, what message are you trying to give Cindy?" The reply was, "Cindy, I am protecting you from being sexual. You don't trust yourself to be able to say 'no'. You are afraid that when you get into a sexual relationship, you become too emotionally involved and then you feel deeply hurt when you break-up." When I asked Cindy to imagine that she was now herself and looking at the inside of the vagina, she said, "It looks healthier." (I notice that the image will always change after you hear or sense the correct information).

Cindy was quite surprised to find out that her yeast infection was actually helping her to succeed in her goal of not getting into another relationship. She laughed as she realized that when she is involved in a loving, committed, intimate relationship, her infection always disappears. Once Cindy was able to trust herself to remain celibate without yeast infections, her condition improved. Her vagina even went on to tell her how to heal it.

I am convinced, after helping many clients, that we have all the answers inside of us, and we have the power to heal ourselves. Our bodies' ailments are giving us important messages about what we are feeling and thinking, and what we need. When we resolve the issue(s) and do the healthy things it asks us to, we can have amazing results.

A third example of how your body problems are trying to give you messages is the case of George, a 55-year-old recovering alcoholic and chain smoker. He came to me to help him feel better about himself so that he could remain sober.

In one of his sessions, George told me he was very concerned about a spot on his lungs that his doctor found on his chest x-ray. I said, "Close your eyes and allow yourself to imagine that you are very small and slipping into your mouth and down into your lung. What are you seeing?" George replied, "I'm seeing a black spot on my lung."

I continued, "George, imagine you are that black spot and you are seeing an image of yourself standing in front of you. Now, as the spot, tell George, "I want you to—and finish the sentence." The black spot went on to tell George that he needed to cut down on his smoking, eat better, and get more rest.

When I then guided George back to being himself and seeing the spot in front of him, he was surprised that it looked smaller and lighter. After George made a commitment to his lung that he would take better care of himself, the spot disappeared.

Then I said, "George, create a way to clean your lungs out." We both laughed as George visualized himself washing out his lungs with a hose. Then he bathed it with a green healing color. I suggested to George that he continue to daily wash out his lungs and fill them with a healing color for a week, as well as encouraged him to do as his lungs requested.

The next month, George was in group therapy and shared this story with us. He said, "I went back to the doctor after I took another x-ray of my lungs. I told my doctor that I knew the spot wasn't there anymore. He asked me how I knew, and I explained to him that I have been washing it down with a hose and bathing it with a green healing color. The expression on the doctor's face told me that he thought I was joking. But he was baffled when the x-ray showed clear lungs. The spot was not there. Very skeptical, he sent me back for another x-ray. To his amazement, once again there were no spots on my lungs. The doctor concluded that the first x-ray must have been defective. There must have been no spot on my lungs to begin with."

We all laughed as we pictured the scene of George, a big, macho man, telling his doctor about his self-healing process. Surely, the doctor did not learn about this phenomenon in medical school. We all congratulated George for his successful healing of his lungs.

Ruth, a forty-two-year-old divorced woman, also had a lot of success improving her health conditions. She was very depressed during and after the Christmas Holidays. Ruth explained to me that this has been a yearly problem for as long as she could remember.

When I asked her to close her eyes and go back to the first time she felt that way, she visualized herself as a little girl in her home during the month of December. Ruth sobbed uncontrollably as she recalled her many painful Christmas times. She realized how all those unexpressed emotions from her childhood years were being triggered every December. She understood why Christmas was such a miserable time of the year for her, even though her parents were long since deceased and she had grown children of her own.

Ruth continued to heal her inner child and replace her negative beliefs with positive ones. She succeeded in raising her self-esteem, and we happily terminated our counseling sessions.

In the month of May, Ruth called me to let me know how excited she was, because for the first time that she could remember, she didn't need any hay fever shots or medication. In fact, she said, "I had a glorious spring and I feel wonderful!"

As this case demonstrates, one cause of allergies is unexpressed emotions of fear, hurt, etc. It was the way Ruth's body was telling her that she had unresolved issues.

Another example is Susan, a fifty-year-old realtor. When Susan first started coming to my office, she always had to have a pillow placed under her arthritic knees when she lay down. It was interesting that when Susan became aware of an emotionally painful issue, she would immediately begin to move her legs around to ease her increasing physical pain. As Susan expressed her anger, fear, resentments, and grief, and she resolved the issue, the pain ceased and her legs became still and relaxed.

By the time we terminated Susan's counseling sessions, she had very little arthritic pain. I reassured her that if she kept dealing with her emotions, her body could continue to heal.

Julie, a thirty-three-year-old woman, had also suffered from arthritis. I wasn't aware of that until I observed something interesting during one of her sessions. I had questioned Julie if she was feeling angry about what her boyfriend had done. As she answered me, I noticed that she stuck her hands into her pockets. When I asked Julie to take her hands out of her pockets, she was surprised to see them in a fist position. Julie's words were, "Oh, so that's where I stuff my anger. No wonder I have arthritis in my fingers."

Stuffing anger can cause serious physical problems, as my client Lori, a young woman in her twenties, also discovered. At her first session, Lori came practically crawling into the office. Her lower back was in so much pain that she could hardly move, stand, or sit. Lori was glad to be able to lie down on the mattress. She was under a doctor's care for her back, but progress was very slow.

I noticed that I often had to ask Lori to repeat herself because she spoke very softly. When she regressed back to her childhood years, we discovered that when Lori's father spanked her, he would hit her even harder if she cried. She always tiptoed around the house and spoke quietly so as not to disturb her short-tempered, angry father.

Needless to say, Lori was furious about all the stifling and the abuse she experienced as a child. But stuck in an old survival pattern, she was terrified to yell out her anger, or cry out her sadness even in the office. In order to survive in her childhood home, Lori felt she needed to always be in control of her emotions. She had great control of her feelings but her young body was suffering greatly.

During the first few individual sessions, Lori wasn't able to let go of her emotions. It was only after she participated in Group Therapy and saw other clients express their feelings in a constructive way—only after she noticed that they felt safe and they even received support from the others—that Lori opened up.

One day, with a broad smile on her face and with a loud and clear voice, Lori shared with the group that she had been able to yell out her anger at her father in her walk-in closet at home, as she beat up a pillow. She also felt safe enough to let herself cry in the darkness and comfort of her little closet. In fact, she let the little girl inside of her sob for about an hour. Soon after that breakthrough, Lori felt complete with therapy. She walked out of my office standing tall and walking with ease as her back was healing.

I have noticed that certain emotions are blocked in specific areas of the body. For example, clients usually discovered hidden anger when they have upper or lower back pain, headaches, and tightness in the base of the skull, or jaw pain. When they constructively release their anger into a pillow, they feel better.

I often find fear blocked in abdominal areas. Sadness is usually stuffed in the sinuses or the sides of the back of the neck. The feeling of responsibility causes tension on the shoulders. Hurt often explains the tightness in the center of the chest, or in the heart area.

I believe that one reason why so many men are stricken with heart disease is because they are brought up not to express their feelings and not to be vulnerable. They are told early on when they express sadness or hurt, "Don't be a sissy. Be a man!"

An example of a stifled man is Tom, a businessman in his forties, who finally came into the office when his wife, Sandy, threatened to leave him. Sandy complained to me in her private sessions that she felt as though she was living with a machine. Tom never expressed his emotions and was critical of Sandy when she expressed hers. Of course, Tom wanted Sandy to be more logical. I found this to be a very common problem for couples who are having difficulties.

Even though Tom came into my office, he was still very resistant. He insisted that he was fine and had no problems. Meeting him on his level and at his comfort zone, I said, "Tom, let's be logical. You are telling me that your childhood was fine and that you have no issues to resolve. But the reality is that you are struggling in your career, you are having serious problems with your daughters and your wife, and you have been warned about the beginnings of heart problems. Let's take the analogy of an automobile. If your car isn't running right, do you believe that nothing is wrong, or do you open up the hood and fix it? Obviously Tom, your life is not running well, which means you have to deal with the issues in your subconscious that are causing you all your problems. In a sense, pick up your hood."

Tom reluctantly realized that I had a point. He finally lay down on the office mattress, loosened his tie and was willing to regress back to his childhood.

Needless to say, there was an incredible amount of pain there. Tom had succeeded in blocking his childhood, and his denial of it was setting him up for disaster. It was amazing to see this logical machine-like person transform into a feeling human being as he expressed his fears, deep hurts, shame, anger, and grief.

Tom, an intelligent, well-dressed man, had deceived himself and everyone else, except his family and his body. Underneath all that calm and apparent self-confidence was a very insecure man harboring an incredible amount of turmoil.

I will never forget the joyful day in the office when Tom completed healing the issues that had been locked in his heart, and he re-owned all of himself, including his feelings. Soon after, he told me about the wonderful report he received from the doctor. Tom felt so good about himself that he began to watch his diet, exercise more, and improve his relationship with his wife and children.

Sarah's story is another example of how important it is to listen to what our bodies are telling us. When Sarah called me for the first time, she related how my book, ***Free to Fly—Dare to Be a Success***, had "jumped out at her" in the bookstore. After she read it, she understood why and wanted to come to see me.

Sarah was in her forties and was suffering from recurring cancer. She shared with me that she had felt pains in her throat for over a year but ignored the symptoms. When she finally did go for medical treatment, the doctors found a malignant tumor in her throat, which they proceeded to remove. Sarah felt optimistic until six months ago, when they discovered a tumor in the back of her neck and in her lower back. Sarah was in severe pain and she wasn't very hopeful.

During the first counseling session, Sarah was able to express her anger, shame, and fears—something she said she never did. She was definitely a placater or people pleaser. Sarah almost always had a smile on her face and tried to make everyone happy.

When Sarah returned the next week, she told me that she was able to cut her pain medication in half. After another session in which she released intensive emotional pain, she was totally free of physical pain.

It wasn't long before the tumors dissolved. However, Sarah called me up one day very upset. She was feeling pain in her throat where the first tumor was removed. I reassured her that the doctors succeeded in removing the cancerous growth, the symptom, but the emotional cause was still unresolved.

The following session, the pain in her throat completely disappeared. I helped Sarah become aware of and release her issues about being afraid to speak up, and about communicating how she really felt.

I have found the body to be very literal. Some examples are: tension in the throat deals with the fear of speaking, problems in the eyes relate to not wanting to see something, and hearing problems correspond to the desire not to hear.

Melinda, a young woman in her early thirties, had many painful ear infections when she was a child. When Melinda regressed back to that time, she became aware that she didn't want to hear because it was too painful for her to listen to her mother's yelling and complaining.

Sidney, a fifty-five-year-old massage therapist, discovered in his counseling sessions that he was losing his hearing because he did not want to hear his wife's nagging.

The body definitely expresses what one is feeling and thinking. People who had tension in their knees found relief when they overcame their negative belief that they couldn't stand on their own two feet. Others expressed their anger by hitting a pillow and had immediate relief from bursitis in their shoulders. They were once again able to raise their arms without pain.

Another interesting phenomenon I have learned about the body is that it will accommodate your belief systems. For example, if the only way you believe you can take time off from work or allow yourself to receive attention from your family is by getting sick or having an accident, you may do just that. Wouldn't it be better to take "well" days rather than "sick" days so that you can enjoy them and let your body be healthy? Vacations are very important for rejuvenation. Instead of letting yourself get sick or have an accident, ask your family for what you want.

This is obvious with children when they keep getting sick to get the time and attention they need, or to avoid having to go to school. If your children are often sick, you may want to pay more loving attention to them when they are well, and help them to talk about and resolve the problems they are having in school.

Amazingly, I've even had clients who realized that they were sick or injured, because they felt guilty. Tonya, a very attractive twenty-one-year-old blonde, had a scar on her forehead from a car accident. Fortunately, her pretty bangs covered it well. I asked Tonya to close her eyes and return to the scene of the accident where a truck hit her car head on. I said, "Tonya, imagine that you are up in the sky and looking down at the collision and tell the Tonya in the car why she created that accident."

She replied, "Tonya, you created that accident because you felt guilty about having so much more than your family members and your friends. You are prettier, smarter, and more successful. And you also didn't appreciate all that you had."

It may be hard to believe, but every time a client of mine had an accident, we always discovered the underlying reasons why she created it. For example, Sylvia burned her thumb when she was trying to light the water heater. When I asked her to observe the incident from above, she said, "Sylvia, you were angry at yourself for not saying 'no' to those people who just showed up without being invited. You didn't want to play hostess or take care of them." Sylvia then realized that she had punished herself for not being true to her feelings.

Are you aware of how you are feeling? Do you express your feelings and thoughts constructively? If you are not, it would be the best health insurance policy you could own. Take the time to deal with your emotions that are expressed in your body. The exercises in Part III can be very helpful.

Your body loves you. Do you love your body? Your body is talking to you. Are you listening?

Chapter 8

"Romantic Relationships 101"

The powerful four-letter word "love", when said or heard, feels so warm and caring. What a delicious experience it is to love and to be loved. In order to succeed in loving relationships, it is important to have a deep understanding of what that word really means, and to know how to open up our hearts and express ourselves in healthy ways. Finally, we need to believe that we deserve precious love, so that we can allow ourselves to experience it in our lives.

Everyone is basically good. I know this because whenever any of my clients did something immoral or destructive, they expressed guilt feelings even if no one ever caught them. I am also convinced that we are all naturally loving. I came to this conclusion when I noticed that after clients released all their anger, fear, and hurt, they instantly began to feel the underlying love that was always there, under their negative feelings, waiting patiently to be allowed to flow.

Many people often had difficulty knowing how they felt, what they wanted to share, and how to express themselves. I look forward to the day when "Romantic Relationships 101" will be a required course in schools, when we will be taught how to become aware of our feelings and to communicate appropriately. What a gift that would be for everyone! It was sad to see couples hurting for many years, because they lacked the necessary tools to build a healthy relationship. (Could you imagine what kind of houses would be built if we had no guidelines or the proper tools?)

The following is a mini course called "Romantic Relationships 101." The goal is to provide you with important insights and solutions to help you experience the successful loving relationships you desire and deserve.

What blocks us from love is our negative thinking. The following positive thoughts can help you create loving relationships. Say, sing, and/or write them until they become a part of you.

Affirmations

1. I forgive myself for all my wrongdoings.
2. I am a good person and I deserve love.
3. I love myself unconditionally.
4. I am offering my love to others unconditionally.
5. I am naturally a loving being.
6. I accept that being loving is the solution.
7. I measure my success of each day by how much I have given and received love to others and myself.
8. I accept that what people say or do is a reflection of them and not of me.
9. I realize that love is my power to heal myself and others.
10. I am opening my heart and choosing to express love.
11. I forgive others who act in hurtful ways because they don't feel lovable or are afraid to love.
12. I am lovable.
13. I am attractive.
14. I am becoming more loving and loved everyday.
15. I am in a wonderful loving relationship with my perfect partner.

Once you are in a loving relationship, the following vows can serve as guidelines for a fantastic relationship.

A Promise of Love

I will:
   Honor your thoughts and feelings.
   Tell you my truth in a loving way.
   Treat you as an equal.
   Accept your uniqueness.

Value the ways we balance each other.
Compliment and appreciate you.
Solve all our conflicts with win-win solutions.
Spend quality time with you.
Continually seek excitement and the magic of life with you.
Love you and myself unconditionally.
Express my deep love for you in many ways.
Cherish you with all my heart.

You now have some general insights into how to succeed in relationships. The following letter will help you deal with more specific issues. It is also helpful to read aloud the appropriate parts to your loving partner and ask him or her to do the same. The goal is to offer the information in a loving way and at a time when your loved one can be receptive.

Dear Love

My dearest partner, I love you very much and I want to have a fantastic relationship with you. Therefore, I am going to give you the gift of telling you my deepest desires.

First of all, my love, I want to thank you for being in my life. I feel honored and privileged that you have chosen me to be your partner. I love and appreciate all the precious times we spend together, as well as all the wonderful things you do for me and allow me to do for you. Thank you for loving me and for sharing yourself in so many ways.

It's no coincidence that I have attracted you into my life. I have deliberately chosen you to help me experience and learn many important lessons. These include how to share and have fun, communicate constructively, and love others and myself unconditionally. Please hear the following as guidelines for our fantastic relationship.

Dear love, please be patient with me and forgive me when I make mistakes. I am human and I am likely to blunder. Understand that I am always doing my best at the time. If I could do differently, I would. Please also be more patient with yourself. Realize that mistakes offer us opportunities to learn. Thank you for being patient with the two of us.

I love when you communicate clearly and specifically so that I can know how you feel and what you want. Expecting me to read your mind, or believing that if I cared about you I would know what you are thinking, often leads to unnecessary hurt and resentment. I appreciate when you take the time to become quiet and tune in to how you are feeling and what you desire, so that you can clearly communicate with me.

Kindly listen to me when I communicate with you. Then I won't want to nag, yell, or withdraw. Thank you for listening to me, because I so much desire to continue to share myself with you.

I also would like you to keep clearing your resentments with me and encourage me to clear my resentments with you, so that we can maintain a loving relationship.

Please release your anger constructively. Anger is a normal human emotion. Accept that it is okay to feel that way and then explore the underlying emotion, which is usually hurt, fear, or powerlessness. When you are clear of the cause of your anger, please calmly share that with me.

I appreciate when you continue to spend time and energy on our relationship and know that we can solve our issues by communicating constructively.

When you become aware of a problem we have, please tell me so that we can resolve it. Let's clearly identify the issue and brainstorm possible solutions. Thank you for helping us to solve our problems with win-win solutions.

I would like you to encourage me to express my deepest fears and doubts. Understand that fear is the bottom-line cause of most of my problems. Listen to my concerns with compassion and understanding. I appreciate when you accept my fears as real, even though they may be irrational. That really helps me face my issues and work on resolving them.

Dear love, please share your deepest fears and doubts with me. If you don't, they can build barriers in our relationship and you are likely to unconsciously act them out in destructive ways. Thank you for having the courage to face your feelings and for sharing your concerns with me.

If I am upset, I would like you to ask me in a loving way what I want and need from you. Sometimes I may want you to just give me the time and space to work it out by myself. Other times, I may need you to just hold me in your arms and tell me you love me. I appreciate when you ask me what I want and need.

Please tell me the truth so that I can trust you. I also need your actions to be consistent with your words. Thank you for being honest with me and for keeping your agreements.

Understand that I may need time alone to rest and relax when I come home from work. When you allow me some space to unwind from the day, it will be easier for me to be there for you.

Please support me when I want to explore my interests, talents, and potential. If you try to hold me back, I am likely to resent you. I believe that we are both here to become all that we can be. Thank you for encouraging me to experience the many facets of my unique self.

I love when you are affectionate and tell me you care about me. Understand that I may need harmony before I can be sexual with you. It is not you I am rejecting; it is our disharmony. Our sexual experiences are often a barometer of how successful we are in expressing our caring and support for each other throughout the day. So please express your love to me in many ways; for example, by hugging, listening, sharing, complimenting, resolving our conflicts and spending quality time with me. Then we can also express our deep caring in a beautiful sexual way.

I like when you tell me what you want sexually and when you encourage me to share with you what I desire. Let's be creative and romantic. Let's have fun and enjoy loving foreplay and holding each other closely after we are sexually satisfied. Thank you for helping to keep our physical expression of our love caring, stimulating, exciting, and fulfilling.

Dear love, please take responsibility for your happiness or negative feelings of discontentment. You are the only one who can truly make you happy. I can contribute to your good feelings by things I say and do. However, since long-lasting happiness can only come from within, please do what you need to do in order to create your own happiness deep inside yourself.

Understand that I am responsible for my happiness. If I feel discontented, please avoid taking responsibility for my feelings and thinking that, "If only I was a better person, my love would be happier." Know that you are okay and help me explore what I need to do in order to feel content.

I appreciate when you share with me the type of relationship you want and encourage me to do the same with you. Together we can develop a mutual understanding of how we want our relationship to be.

When we design our relationship to fit our specific needs and wants, we have a better chance of succeeding. There is no right or wrong ways of doing things. What's appropriate for us at the time is what's important for us to discuss. We are likely to experience many problems and pain if we focus on who we think we should be and what we think should be happening. Thank you for sharing with me how you truly want our relationship to be.

Sometimes I may want to spend some time alone so that I can nurture my relationship with myself. Please don't see my behavior as a rejection of you. When I have a better relationship with myself, I am more able to have a fantastic one with you.

My dearest partner, I would like you to let go of any hurtful feelings and thoughts that you have with members of your family and past lovers. If you don't, you are likely to project those negative feelings onto me. It is hard for you to see who I really am, if you have unfinished business with others. The truth is that your family and ex-lovers did the best they could and never meant you any harm. If they acted in a negative way towards you, it was because they were hurting inside with feelings that had nothing to do with you. Please find it in your heart to forgive them. Thank you for clearing your unfinished business and your old perceptions of relationships, so that you can really see and relate to me.

Please forgive yourself for all your wrongdoings. If you don't, your guilt feelings may cause you to sabotage your health, happiness, and success. Punishing yourself hurts you and me. Thank you for releasing your guilt feelings and forgiving yourself so that you can accept the truth that you are a good person and you do deserve a fantastic relationship.

Dear love, I would like you to appreciate my uniqueness and avoid any competition with me. I may feel resentful if you try to prove to me that you are better. See me as your teammate and encourage me to be the best I can be, so that we can both be winners.

Please trust me to be faithful. If you are jealous or possessive, I may feel controlled, caged-in, and resentful. Jealousy is often caused by feelings of inadequacy. Accept that you are good enough and that I am committed to you and our relationship. And thank you for being committed to me.

I want you to help me feel equally powerful. I am likely to resent you if you try to have control over me ~ that is, you want to feel dominant or superior. Pure power is found inside of you when you are loving yourself, being who you are, and doing what you want to do. So if you feel the need to have control over me, please turn inward and focus on taking charge of your life and help me do the same with mine.

Dear partner, let's play together. We both need to have fun in order to get re-energized and enjoy life, and I love to play with you. Let's continue to seek excitement, fun, and the magic of life with each other.

If you feel you are not getting your needs met, I would like you to share your discontent with me. If you seek other relationships to satisfy yourself, you will hurt both of us. Please give me the opportunity to explore with you what you want and need so that we can improve our relationship.

If you think that I am not hearing your discontent, encourage me to go with you for professional help. A counselor can help us improve our communication and resolve our problems. If I feel frustrated and unable to reach you with my wants and needs, please agree to go with me for professional assistance. It is a sign of courage and strength to know when we need to reach out for help. Thank you for doing everything you can in order to make our relationship all that it can be.

If I am addicted to food, alcohol, or drugs, understand that these are only the symptoms ~ the tip of the iceberg. The underlying cause is my low self-esteem. With sensitivity and compassion, encourage me to explore the emotional pain that I am trying to stuff with food, drown with alcohol, or numb with drugs. Help me release my feelings in constructive ways. Thank you for being understanding and supportive so that I can raise my self-esteem and be in control of my life.

Dear love, know that you deserve to be treated with kindness and respect. If I am physically or verbally abusive, please don't tolerate that destructive behavior. No matter what happens, you do not deserve to be the target of my emotional pain. See that destructive behavior as a projection of how I feel about myself. If I am not willing to hear your protests, or seek professional help, then do what you have to do in order to protect yourself. If you let me get away with my destructive, hurtful behavior, I'm likely to continue to be in emotional pain and keep hurting you. Thank you for encouraging me to constructively deal with my pain and for not allowing me to be abusive to you. Thank you for understanding that what I do or say is a reflection of me and not of you.

Let's balance our lives between work and play. Then we will be better able to deal with the normal frustrations of life and avoid burnout. When we balance our four parts ~ mental, physical, emotional, and spiritual ~ we will be happier and healthier, individually and together.

Please take care of your health. I care about you and I want you to be my partner and enjoy things with me for a very long time. Think positively, exercise regularly, and eat healthy foods. Keep yourself attractive and encourage me to do the same. That is important for our self-esteem. It also helps us to continue to desire each other.

If we have children, understand that we need special time alone in order to nurture our relationship. Our healthy, intimate relationship helps us cope with the normal stresses of a family. If we make our relationship a priority, we are likely to be more patient parents and wonderful models for our children. They will be learning from our words and behavior how to create their own fantastic relationships. Realize that when they are grown we need to let them go. If we keep nurturing our relationship, we can look forward to those precious years of being just a couple again.

Dear partner, I appreciate when you give to me unconditionally. I may feel resentful if I think that you are keeping score, or giving to me with the expectation of receiving. It feels wonderful to receive from you when you give for the joy of giving. Also allow me the gift of giving to you. Thank you for seeing giving and receiving as a natural flow ~ like the ocean tide flowing in and out.

Realize that the biggest gift you give to me is yourself. I support you in your career and appreciate all the material things you offer me, the clean house, and delicious meals. However, know that nothing can replace the most precious gift of loving time together. Thank you for being there for me emotionally as well as physically.

Let's be best friends. That is, share our feelings and ideas, do things together, admire, respect, and like one another. When we treat each other as we would our best friends, we have a wonderful basis for a healthy relationship. Add that to our romantic feelings and expressions of caring and we can experience a fantastic relationship.

Please accept me the way I am. I may be different from you and I am okay. In fact, the way we complement each other is probably one reason why we are together. Thank you for accepting me even though you don't always understand me.

Love me unconditionally. That means that you love all of me, all of the time, even though you may not always like or agree with what I am doing or saying. Loving me in that way becomes easier as you love yourself unconditionally.

Let's work on raising our self-esteem. When we both feel self-confident, we have strong foundations for our bridge, which is symbolic of our relationship. With high self-esteem and constructive communication, we can deal with life's many lessons and continue to stand strong and proud.

Let's live in the present and enjoy every moment. Now is all there is. Let's learn from our past, set our goals for the future and live in the precious now. I would like us to cherish our time together, quiet our minds, and open up our hearts. Let's surrender to love and make it our main focus and highest priority. Our success of each day is not measured by how much we did, but how much we loved.

Let's walk life together, side-by-side, and enjoy the journey, including the challenges, and support each other along the way ~ always knowing that our number-one goal is to love each other and ourselves unconditionally. Let's understand that whatever the problem, love is the answer. Then we will experience incredible joy, health, and unlimited success and happiness.

Thank you for hearing me. I love you!

Congratulate yourself for being willing to constructively share your needs and wants with your loving partner.

The following insights and solutions offer you a summary of what you just read as well as more guidelines to help you create a healthy relationship.

I noticed that my clients often had similar needs and did not know how to express their desires in a positive way. In order to help them to communicate, I gave each client the following lists, and I asked them both to check-off what they wanted to say to their partner. Then they exchanged lists, read what their lover requested, and expressed whether or not they were willing to give them what they wanted. Most of the time, because they loved each other and really wanted their partner to be happy, they were more than willing to do what was requested. In fact, they shared how glad they were to receive clear messages.

If one of them was not willing to honor a request, then we resolved the issue with Win-Win Problem Solving. (Note the chapter on Empowering Communication.)

To help you have the fantastic relationship you desire, you may want to do the same with your partner. Take the time to check-off what you both want, and give each other the gift of communicating honestly and constructively.

Dear Love

Please...

Accept me the way I am. That helps me know that I'm okay even though I'm different from you.

Allow me time to rest when I come home from work. That helps me unwind from the day and be able to be there for you.

Spend quality time with me. That helps me feel I'm important to you.

Compliment and appreciate me. That helps me feel acknowledged and then I want to continue to please you.

Help me to explore my unique interests, talents, and potential. That helps me to feel supported, happy, and fulfilled.

Forgive yourself for all your wrongdoings. Then you'll allow yourself to enjoy a wonderful relationship with me.

Balance your life between work and play. That helps me do the same and then we can have more precious times together.

Realize that I'm responsible for my life. Then you'll know you're okay and good enough no matter how I feel, or what I do or say.

Be affectionate and tell me you love me. That helps me feel lovable and loving.

Continue to seek excitement, fun, and the magic of life with me. Then we can maintain a fantastic relationship.

Thank you for listening to me. I love you!

Dear Loving Partner

Please...

Communicate your thoughts and feelings clearly and specifically. That helps me know what you want and need.

Listen to me. Then I'll feel heard and want to communicate with you.

Keep clearing your resentments. Then we can continue to feel close and loving.

Release your anger constructively and then tell me calmly what you're angry about and if you feel hurt or scared. Then we can resolve the issue and both feel good.

Help me solve our problems with win-win solutions. Then we can maintain a healthy relationship.

Keep your agreements and tell me the truth. Then I can trust you.

Be patient with me and forgive me when I make mistakes. That helps me know that I'm okay even when I blunder.

Take responsibility for all your feelings and behavior. That helps me know that I'm only responsible for my feelings and behavior.

Trust and respect me. That helps me feel good when I'm with you.

Treat me as you would your best friend. That helps me know that you like and love me.

Thank you for hearing me. I love you!

Dear Lover

Please...

Be romantic and affectionate. That helps me feel loved and loving.

Understand that I need harmony before I can be sexual with you. It's not you I'm rejecting; it's our disharmony.

Realize the importance of loving foreplay and after-play. That helps me feel nurtured and fulfilled.

Focus on my whole body and tell me how much you care. That helps me feel you love all of me.

Be patient and accept that whatever happens is okay. Without pressure or expectations, we can relax and enjoy our sexuality.

Communicate what you desire and encourage me to do the same. Then we'll be able to please each other.

Be satisfied sometimes just by kissing or holding each other. Then I'll know we can be loving and intimate also in nonsexual ways.

Understand that I'm responsible for my feelings. That helps me feel okay and good enough even if I don't climax.

Explore with me new ways to express our sexual desires. Then we can continue to enjoy a fun and exciting love life.

Cherish your sexuality as another wonderful way of demonstrating your love. That helps me feel you're making love to me (coming from your heart).

Thank you for hearing me. I love you!

When I'm Upset

Please...

Be patient with me.

Know that I'm responsible for all my emotions.

Accept that my feelings are okay even though they may be irrational.

Wait until I'm calm before you approach me.

Ask me if I'm ready to talk about it.

Listen to me and try to understand the way I'm feeling.

Comfort me.

Help me overcome my fears and solve the problems.

Be kind and loving.

Encourage me to see the humor in the situation.

Thank you for caring. I love you!

When You're Upset

Please...

Take responsibility for all your feelings.

Do something constructive to calm yourself down. For example, take a walk, listen to soothing music, or write about what happened.

Tell me when you are ready to discuss it.

Share with me your hurt, fear, or concerns.

Allow me to comfort you.

Know that you're okay no matter what anyone says or does.

See what you can learn from the experience.

Explore ways to solve the problem.

Be able to laugh at the situation.

Congratulate yourself for dealing with your upset in a healthy way.

Thank you for hearing me. I love you!

When We're Upset

Please let's...

Avoid hurting each other or ourselves.

Separate and do something to calm ourselves down.

Realize that we are responsible for all our feelings and behavior.

Explore the fear or hurt that caused the upset.

Meet again when we are calm and clear about our feelings.

Share our perceptions of the event.

Listen to each other.

Apologize if we feel it is appropriate.

Solve the problem with a win-win solution.

Learn from our upset and become closer.

Thank you for hearing me. I love you!

When I Have a Problem

Please...

Tell me that you are there for me. That helps me know that you care.

Ask me if I would like to discuss my problem. Then you'll know whether I'm ready to resolve it.

Listen to what I'm saying and tell me in your own words what you heard. Then I'll know that you are hearing me.

Accept my feelings even if you do not understand them. That helps me feel my emotions are valid even if they are irrational.

Share with me if you also felt that way. Then I'll know that you can relate to me.

Explain what you would do in my situation. Then I'll see some possible solutions.

Ask me what my choices are. That helps me think of some other alternatives.

Help me brainstorm all possible resolutions. Then I'll have many creative ideas.

Suggest that I write down the pros and cons of my decisions. That helps me clarify my thoughts.

Encourage me to write down the details of my solutions. That helps me put them into action.

Thank you for being patient, accepting, and supportive. I love you!

When You Have a Problem

Please...

Know that it is solvable.

See it as an opportunity to learn something.

Explore your problem alone by completing the sentences: My problem is ____. Or, I feel ____.

Realize that asking me for support is a gift to me. You are demonstrating that you are human and that you too have problems.

Ask me when we can meet to discuss your issue.

Tell me about how much time we will need.

Be clear whether you want me to just listen or help you solve the problem.

Share with me specifically how I can help you.

Be patient with yourself and me.

Compliment yourself for having the courage to reach out to me.

Thank you for trusting me. I love you!

When We Have a Problem

Please let's...

Know that we can resolve it.

Realize it is an opportunity for both of us to learn something and be closer.

Separately express all our emotions in constructive ways. For example, release our anger into a soft pillow and explore any hurt, fear, or powerless feelings.

Decide on a specific time when we can meet to resolve the issue.

State the agreed on problem in the form of a question. For example, "How can we spend more time together?"

Brainstorm by writing down all possible solutions without either one commenting.

Narrow down the suggestions by taking turns crossing off any we prefer to eliminate, without giving any reasons.

Both state the mutually accepted solution(s).

Work out the details together.

Plan on a follow-up date to meet again to see if the problem has been resolved.

**Thank you for helping to create win-win solutions.
I love you!**

Seven Keys to a Great Relationship

1. **I am ready to create what I want in a relationship.**
   Become clear about what you want in your relationship. Then share your thoughts with your partner. Know that you are powerful enough to have what you desire and that you deserve it.
2. **I am my own best friend and I am responsible for my own life and happiness.**
   Love and like yourself and look to your relationship as the icing on the cake. Know that you are whole and complete by yourself and that you are the only one who can bring you lasting happiness.
3. **I am learning to communicate clearly, specifically and constructively.**
   Take the time to communicate with yourself so that you can clearly tell your partner how you feel and what you want and need. Remember that you are responsible for all of your emotions and that you are okay no matter what your partner says or does.
4. **I am letting go of hurtful thoughts and feelings from my past relationships.**
   Heal your past issues with your parents, siblings, and other loved ones. Then you will be able to clearly see your partner for who he or she really is.

5. **I am continually seeking excitement, fun, and the magic of life with my partner.**
   Be romantic and explore different activities that you and your partner can enjoy. Create new ways to have fun and to keep your relationship alive and stimulating. For example, schedule weekly date nights.

6. **I am encouraging my partner and myself to explore and develop our individual potentials.**
   Both you and your loved one will be a lot happier when you become all that you are. It takes two happy people to make a happy, successful relationship.

7. **I love and accept my partner and myself unconditionally.**
   Focus on unconditionally loving yourself and then you will be able to offer the same true love to your partner. Unconditional love means heartfelt caring and kindness even though you may not approve of an action. It is an important key to health, happiness, success, and a fantastic relationship.

A Degree in Intimacy

Now you have many guidelines, insights, and solutions. I suggest that you continue to explore ways to be more loving and successful in your relationships. Make "A Degree in Intimacy" a priority in your life. The truth is that you deserve love, and that you have the power to create the fulfilling relationship that you desire.

Chapter 9

Enjoy Your Sexuality

*H*ave you ever wondered what causes our sexual problems? Are you curious why so many people do not enjoy their sexuality?

I noticed that many clients were struggling with sexual issues that were also affecting other areas of their lives. In many cases, they felt guilty for not wanting to be sexual or even for enjoying it. Men and women often felt inadequate in their lovemaking and experienced high levels of anxiety that lowered their self-esteem.

The troubling feelings also affected their relationships. In some cases, it prevented them from allowing themselves to engage in a loving partnership. Very often, their unfulfilling sexual experiences with their lover or spouse caused them to have many arguments, a break-up, or divorce.

It would be wonderful if we all received the necessary education and positive guidance to understand and enjoy our sexuality. Most of us learned about sex from our parents, siblings, or friends. They could only share with us what they had learned from others. Unfortunately, it was probably inaccurate and negative. That is because sexual taboos have been passed on for many generations.

Many times, nothing was ever said about sex. The conclusion from this experience could also easily be *sex must be bad*.

The other common problem is that many people do not know how to have a fulfilling sexual experience. It is true that we have an instinct to be sexual, but we are not born great lovers. Making love is another whole experience that is usually learned.

Could you relate to any of these issues? How did you learn about sex?

Before we explore sexual issues, I would like to clarify my terms. Often the word "sex" describes only physical contact with our erogenous, sexual parts. That is what animals do instinctively.

However, lovemaking includes physical and emotional interaction. That is, coming from deep caring or love. Being sexual is another way we give and receive pleasure with someone we care about. It is another way to express our love. When I refer to sex, I also mean lovemaking.

It has been a joy to help many men and women overcome their emotional sexual blocks and enjoy their physical, healthy expression of caring.

The first client that comes to my mind is Susan, a twenty-two-year-old woman, who was not enjoying her sexual experience with her boyfriend. The young lady was not convinced that she had a problem, but Fred had encouraged her to see me. A sensitive person, Fred was aware that Susan was just being sexual to please him. He was feeling frustrated and unhappy. He told her that part of his pleasure was feeling that she was also enjoying their lovemaking.

Susan went on to explain, "At first, Fred accused me of not caring about him. After I convinced him how much I do love him, he was depressed because he then thought that he was not a good lover. I reassured him that he was great, but I had never enjoyed sex, not even with my previous boyfriends." "Helene, do women really enjoy sex?" Susan asked. I replied, "Susan, do you allow yourself to enjoy your sense of hearing, sight, smell, touch, and taste?"

"Of course I do," Susan answered, "but that is different." I continued, "In my opinion, we would not have sensual bodies if we were not supposed to enjoy them. Our sexual parts, just like our eyes, ears, nose, skin, and tongue, are normal parts of us that have specific functions, as well as offer us specific pleasures."

Susan looked surprised at my response, but she saw my point. I went on to reassure her that sex was a normal, healthy part of a relationship—another way to express love and give and receive pleasure. I reassured her that enjoying her sexuality is a natural state—that she probably made negative decisions about sex from her childhood experiences that were still affecting her today.

Susan looked puzzled as she said, "But I don't remember anything bad happening to me in that way." I asked her if she was willing to close her eyes and let me guide her through the HART process so that she could find her answers and resolve the issues.

Skeptical, but curious, Susan closed her eyes and allowed herself to breathe deeply a few times to relax. I then began to guide her to her answers by saying, "Susan, allow yourself to visualize the word "sex" written in the sky. How big are the letters?" She replied, "Not very big. In fact, they look pretty small, like they are very far away from me." I then suggested to Susan that she say the words, "Sex means to me ___" and finish the sentence. She said, "Sex means to me something bad, something you tolerate for the sake of a man."

I continued, "Allow yourself to go back to the time when you made that decision about sex." Susan visualized herself when she was ten years old. Her mother was talking on the kitchen telephone. As Susan was walking past the kitchen, she overheard her mother saying, "I just tolerate sex for my husband's sake." Susan continued to walk into the living room and never told her mother what she overheard.

Neither her parents nor her older brother had ever said anything to Susan about sex. But that told her a lot. Her young mind had already decided that it must be bad if no one talks about it. And now this comment from her mother convinced her that sex must be just tolerable and only for a man to enjoy.

In order to release these negative decisions, I suggested to Susan that she tell the image of her mother, "Mom, I am sorry that you did not allow yourself to enjoy your sexuality. I imagine that you just passed on to me the negative messages that your mother impressed on you. The truth is that sex between two consenting adults is a beautiful way to share their love. I accept that you did not know that, but I do. I am going to allow myself to enjoy my sexuality." I noticed an immediate rise in Susan's chest as she automatically took a deep breath of relief. When I asked her how she was feeling, she responded, "More relaxed."

Susan continued to get in touch with and overcome her negative associations with sex. She felt wonderful after she accepted that masturbation was normal and healthy. She realized that since she was a young child she had felt guilty about masturbating and giving herself pleasure. Her guilt feelings caused her to punish herself by not allowing herself to enjoy her sexual experiences with men.

It is interesting that Susan never saw anyone masturbate or learned anything about it. But she somehow knew to touch her genitals only under the covers in the privacy of her own bedroom, and she knew not to tell anyone because it was unacceptable. The young lady was very relieved when I told her that most people masturbated and unfortunately had the same guilt feelings.

As Susan overcame her negative beliefs about her sexuality, she noticed that the word "sex" written in the sky looked bigger and seemed to be closer to her. When she started to associate sex with only positive thoughts, I knew that she had succeeded in overcoming her sexual blocks.

The following week, Susan and Fred came into the office together to improve their communication skills. I explained to them how important it was to always express in a loving way what they liked and what did not feel good. This was especially true during their lovemaking. I said, "When you go into a restaurant, you probably do not assume your partner wants the same thing that he or she ordered the week before. You probably ask your lover what he or she would like now. It is helpful to do the same before, during, and after your sexual experience."

The young couple was grateful for the information. They both smiled as they told me how much better their sexual experiences were. Susan said, "Helene, it feels wonderful to be open to enjoying my sexuality."

Another person who was not allowing himself to enjoy his sexuality by not reaching a climax was a forty-seven-year-old divorced man. When I had counseled Bob six months before, he had succeeded in raising his self-esteem and overcoming his hurt and depression from his divorce.

Bob informed me that he was in a new relationship and that he was able to have an erection, but he could not climax. He said that he was not concerned, but his girlfriend was; she had insisted that he come in to see me.

I knew that Bob had all the answers inside of him. Therefore, I guided him through a process I call "Bull's Eye Sex Therapy". I said, "Bob, close your eyes and relax. Now imagine that you are inside your penis and you are looking out and seeing your girlfriend's vagina coming towards you. What do you want to say to it?"

Bob yelled, "I won't come, you Bitch! This is the one and only place I have control over you!" Bob opened up his eyes, looked at me and said, "Whoa! I had no idea that was there."

Bob realized that there was a part of him that wanted to hold back and that was exactly what he did. His conscious mind was not aware of what he was unconsciously doing. I suggested to Bob that he deal with his resentment in a more constructive way—by resolving the problem of control in their relationship. Then he would be able to allow himself and his partner to fully enjoy their sexual experiences.

Brian, a tall, charming, handsome, thirty-four year old man also had a sexual problem. Even though he attracted many women into his life, he could not maintain a relationship because he was impotent.

In his counseling sessions, Brian discovered that he felt devastated when his wife left him for another man. He had been impotent ever since his divorce. Brian was terrified to get too close to another woman. He never wanted to hurt like that again. His impotency was actually helping him keep his distance—to stay safe.

Unfortunately, Brian was staying safe but not satisfied. His heart truly desired to be in a healthy, loving relationship. But his unconscious fear of intimacy caused his impotency. In order to help Brian to overcome his blocks to relationships, I guided him back to the times his heart was hurt. He released his pain with his mother, sister, other lovers, and ex-wife.

Then I helped Brian become aware of what he did that contributed to the divorce. He realized that he projected onto his wife the negative feelings he had with previous females. Brian then began to feel more hopeful that he could have a more successful marriage in the future.

One of the important lessons he had learned was that providing a big house, two beautiful cars, expensive clothes, and jewelry are not enough to sustain a relationship. Brian admitted that he, like his Dad, was so busy making money that he was rarely home. He had made the serious mistake of not hearing his wife's pleas for more time with him. She was willing to have fewer materialistic things.

Since Brian did so well in therapy, it was no surprise to me when six months later he called to inform me about his engagement. He had succeeded in overcoming his fear of intimacy and was no longer impotent. Brian was now able to enjoy a healthy relationship.

Another man dealing with impotency was Steve, a very successful, tall, broad, fifty-five-yea- old man. A year earlier, he had lost his wife, Peggy, to cancer. Since then he had struggled with impotency.

Steve was now in a new relationship, and he wanted to function normally again. I asked him to close his eyes and relax with a few deep breaths. Then I guided him to imagine that he was inside his penis and to tell me what he saw. Steve said that it looked healthy.

Then I said, "Steve, imagine that you are your penis and you are seeing an image of yourself in front of you. As the penis, tell Steve why he can not get an erection." The penis replied, "I am punishing you for pushing yourself on your sick wife a year and a half ago." (This is an example of the mind/body connection. The troubled body part is often expressing an emotional issue.)

"Allow yourself to go back to the time this happened," I continued. Steve described the very painful, traumatic time. Peggy was sick with cancer. Driven by love and desire, he pushed himself on her sexually. Afterwards, Peggy cried in pain. Steve realized what he had done and felt terrible.

When I asked him what he is deciding from this experience, he said, "I will not be sexual. I never want to do that terrible thing again. I deserve to be punished." Steve realized that he had succeeded in punishing himself. Since that painful event, he was impotent.

In order to help Steve resolve his problem, I said, "Imagine that Peggy is standing in front of you. What do you want to say to her?" Steve cried as he asked Peggy for forgiveness.

I then asked Steve to imagine that he was Peggy and to see an image of himself standing in front of him. Then I said, "Peggy, what do you want to say to Steve?" She replied, "I do forgive you. You can stop punishing yourself. It is okay to go on with your life and experience other fulfilling relationships. I love you, Steve, and I want you to be happy. I would rest more comfortably in peace knowing that you are not alone."

I guided Steve to become himself again and to see Peggy in front of him. I asked him if he was willing to accept her forgiveness and stop punishing himself. Steve said he was. Then I placed a teddy bear on his chest to represent Peggy and I encouraged him to hug her and say, "I love you and I need to let you go." When he stopped sobbing, I gently removed the teddy bear from his chest.

Then I encouraged Steve to forgive himself. Once again I placed the teddy bear on his chest and suggested that it was a part of him. He hugged himself and I encouraged him to say, "I forgive you. I love you. You are a good person. You deserve to feel good."

Steve spontaneously took a deep breath and told me that he felt a great sense of relief. Then I suggested that he visualize a successful sexual experience with his girlfriend. Since Steve was able to do that, I knew that he had healed himself.

At the end of the hour session, I encouraged him to enjoy himself and to let me know if there were any more problems. A month later, Steve called me to tell me about his success. It is exciting to know that there is one more potent man out there, able to share his love also in a sexual way.

It is also exciting to know that there is one healthier woman out there enjoying her sexuality. Pat, a twenty-year-old nurse, came to me complaining that sex with her boyfriend, Tim, was painful. When I asked Pat to close her eyes and look inside her vagina, she said it looked black. I continued, "Pat, imagine that you are inside your vagina and you are seeing Tim's penis coming towards you. What do you want to say to it?" Pat replied, "I am afraid of you hurting me, Tim. I will not let you in. All you want is my body."

I then asked Pat to go back to the time she felt that way before. She regressed back to her college dorm room. Pat had finally given in to be sexual with her boyfriend, John. It was not easy for her, because her father had always told her to be careful. "Men will want you for your beautiful body," he sternly expressed to his daughter.

After that one sexual experience, John broke off with her. She felt devastated. With my support and encouragement, Pat visualized John in front of her. She then expressed to him all of her feelings—her hurt, fears, and anger. When Pat felt relaxed, she changed the scene to be the way she wanted it to be. She heard John say, "Pat, I want all of you!" She also realized that she was enjoying the sex. Then Pat imagined that her father was standing in front of her, and he was smiling with approval.

When Pat returned to her present situation, she was able to begin to believe that Tim loved her completely and that it was okay for her to enjoy her sexuality. I encouraged Pat to say her new positive thoughts everyday for about a month. "I, Pat, am beginning to accept that my boyfriend loves all of me. I, Pat, am beginning to believe that it is okay for me to enjoy my sexuality." Reinforcing her new positive beliefs in this way will help her vagina to relax, so that she could feel pleasure instead of pain.

At the next session, Pat reported that for the first time intercourse was not painful. After a few more counseling sessions, she excitedly shared that sex with Tim felt wonderful.

Eli, a forty-three-year-old professional woman, was also able to overcome her issues and enjoy her sexuality. She told me that she loved her husband dearly but did not enjoy their lovemaking. "I love the touching, holding, and closeness. I love giving to him and seeing him receiving pleasure. But I just do not feel much around my genitals, and I never reach a climax."

I asked Eli to close her eyes, breathe deeply, and relax. Then I guided her to explore her vagina. Eli said, "It looks dark." I continued, "Imagine that you are your vagina and see an image of yourself standing in front of you. Vagina, tell Eli what message you are trying to give her." The vagina replied, "You are bad." Then I said, "Go back to the time when you decided that you are bad and be there now."

Eli returned to the scene when she was five years old. She was in a barn with a little boy. Normally curious, they were exploring each other's bodies. Suddenly, the door opened and her mother stormed into the barn screaming at them, "You are bad, bad children!"

The scared little girl was sent to her room, haunted by the words, "You are a bad girl. Don't you ever do that again!" When Elli's mother told the boy's parents what had happened, they were horrified and punished him with a beating.

When I asked Eli how she was feeling, she replied, "I feel confused. I don't understand why I was bad. I was not doing anything wrong. It felt good. But I must be bad if Mom says I am."

From that traumatic experience, Eli decided that it is bad to feel pleasure in her sexual parts. I continued, "If you are ready to release that negative belief, imagine that you are burning that painful scene away with a laser beam. Then create the scene as you would like it to be."

Eli visualized herself in the barn with the little boy and having fun. I guided her to imagine that her adult self came into the barn and told both children that what they were doing was okay. She also told them that it was normal to be curious and to explore each other and that it was okay to feel good when they touched their genitals. She reassured them that they were good children. Based on this new experience, Eli felt better. She decided that she is a good girl and it is okay to feel pleasure in her sexual parts.

Then I guided Eli to imagine that she was back inside her vagina and to tell me how it looked. To her surprise, she saw a very different looking vagina. It was no longer dark. In fact, it was light. I explained to Eli that the previous dark image was symbolic of the fears and the light image meant that she had overcome her negative beliefs.

Eli smiled and was very pleased. Then I said, "Imagine that you are looking out of your vagina and your husband's penis is coming towards you. What do you want to say to it?" Eli excitedly replied, "Come on in. I am ready to enjoy you!" She went on to visualize a wonderful sexual experience with her husband, including orgasm.

When Eli returned the following week, I asked her if there were any changes in her sexual experiences. She replied, "I did enjoy sex more than ever, but I have not experienced an orgasm." I congratulated Eli on her success and reassured her that she will experience a climax when she is ready to allow herself to enjoy her sexuality to the fullest.

The most challenging sexual issues I have helped clients overcome are those of childhood molestation and incest. Although I assisted men who had experienced this form of abuse, the majority of cases were women.

Cathy, a forty-year-old woman, had sexual intercourse with her Dad from the time she was six until she was sixteen years old. It stopped only because she eloped with her boyfriend to get out of the house. Other women I counseled uncovered memories of molestation by their uncles, grandfathers, brothers, stepfathers, a parent's friend, and neighbors.

I was amazed how often these issues came up in the process of healing the inner child. The women often had no conscious memory of the event. They had blocked it, because it was too painful and confusing. But they could not deny it when they regressed back to their childhood, visualized the actual scene and felt scared, hurt, angry, and sad.

Even if the women remembered their molestations, I was often the first one they had ever told. Imagine keeping that secret well into their adult years. They shared it with no one, not even their husbands, but the memories of those traumatic experiences and their negative decisions were still haunting them.

I found that most sexually abused women had felt too scared to tell anyone when they were little girls. Some of them had the courage to tell their mothers. However, because their mothers' egos could not deal with the idea that their boyfriends or husbands would sexually approach their child instead of them, they went into denial and did nothing to protect their daughters. Then the girls also felt betrayed by their mothers.

I discovered that most women had guilt feelings because they felt they must have caused it to happen. In some cases they also had guilt feelings because it felt good. But they all knew that it was wrong. Many of them felt shame and decided that they were bad, dirty, and defective.

Most of the women had an unconscious fear of men, and they felt terrified that they did not have the power to say, "No". All of the women were furious at the perpetrators for victimizing them. They often did not trust men and they projected their anger onto other males.

Obviously, with all these feelings and negative decisions, the women had sexual problems. It was a wonderful experience for me to have the opportunity to help these clients let go of their buried memories, to release their painful emotions, and to change their negative decisions to positive ones. It was wonderful to see the relief on their faces and to know that they would be able to enjoy their sexuality and experience healthy relationships.

Chapter 10

Successful Parenting

*W*e often learn how to parent from the way our mothers, fathers, guardians, or other relatives treated us. Unfortunately, they often learned from their parents and so on through the generations. Therefore, our unconscious dysfunctional patterns are passed on to our children. For example, it has been found that abused children often become abusive mothers and fathers.

It is interesting to note that parenting is a very big responsibility and yet we often do not learn what our children truly need and want. It would be nice if they arrived with a manual. However, since they do not, it is helpful to learn what it takes to be a successful parent. I would love to see required parenting classes in high schools and colleges.

I believe that our parenting role is to take care of our boys and girls physically, mentally, spiritually, and emotionally. We need to help the children have high self-esteem, be their unique selves and prepare them for life.

The following healthy guidelines can help you be a successful parent. Imagine that you are receiving this letter from your child, whether you are the parent, grandparent, guardian, relative, or stepparent.

Dear Mom/Dad,

I love you and I know that you want to be the best parent that you can be. So I am giving you the gift of sharing what I want and need.

I first want to thank you for being my parent. I so much appreciate you for giving birth to me and providing for all my physical needs ~ food, clothing, and a home. Without you, I wouldn't be able to survive. Thank you for taking care of me when I am sick, bandaging me when I am hurt, wiping my tears away when I cry and for all the wonderful things you do for me. I am honored to have you as my parent.

Mom / Dad, I need to believe that you want me, that you also feel honored to have the opportunity to nurture and to guide me. I want you to realize how sensitive I am, even when I am in your womb and especially when I am very young. I, like you, make unconscious decisions based on my experiences ~ what I see, hear, and feel. Therefore, when you are being positive, I can make a positive decision about others and myself. And, of course the opposite is also true.

For example, when you are acting loving towards me, I decide from that experience that I am lovable and I behave in a loving way. You are modeling for me how to be in the world. If you are respectful and caring to others and me, I will also be respectful and caring. What you think, do and say greatly influences me. So please be the person you want me to be.

Dear Mom, if I am still in your womb, please talk lovingly to me and be good to yourself because then you are taking care of the two of us. Know that whatever you are doing, thinking, or feeling is also affecting me.

Please arrange to have my birth experience to be a gentle, nurturing transition from your warm, protective, loving womb into your warm, loving arms. A traumatic experience can cause me to believe that this is an unsafe, cruel world. I do hear what people are saying, so please make sure that I am surrounded by positive people, including those who are assisting my birth and looking after me.

Mom / Dad, the first five years of my life are especially important, because it is a time when I am making many decisions about others, the world, and myself. These unconscious decisions are forming my basic personality. So please help me make positive decisions by providing many positive experiences for me.

For example, when you give me positive attention, I decide that I am worthy and important. When you consistently take care of all my needs, I can begin to trust people and believe that I can depend on them. When you give me little tasks that I can do and acknowledge my accomplishments, I can decide that I am good enough and intelligent. Remember that these decisions are my life script or programming and they determine my behavior.

Dear Mom/Dad, I know that you want me to do the right thing. In fact, I need you to teach me right from wrong. If I make a mistake, please bend down to my level, (when you tower over me, I get scared and it is hard for me to hear you). Then, when we are eye-to-eye, gently tell me that you love me, that I am okay, and that you don't want me to do what I did because of the following reasons.

Please don't yell or hit me. That does more harm than good. If you do punish me, then I decide that you don't love me and that I am a bad person. That negative thought deeply hurts me, because if I think that I am bad, I decide that I don't deserve to be happy and successful. This negative belief causes me many problems as a child and as an adult in my relationships, health, and career.

For example, I may push away a person who cares about me or turn down a good opportunity, because I feel I don't deserve love and success. I also may punish myself by having accidents or getting sick. So please help me decide that I am a good person.

Dear Mom/Dad, there are no victims. I, like you, am totally responsible for everything that happens or doesn't happen to me. It is true that my experiences with you help me to make decisions that affect my life. However, I am still responsible for the decisions I make. I know that you want to help me make the most positive decisions, such as, I am okay, I am good and I deserve to be happy, healthy, and successful. With these beliefs programming me, I can have high self-esteem and do very well in the world.

Please help me learn from my mistakes by first telling me what you want instead of what you don't want. For example, if I am yelling, it is very helpful to me if you say, "Please speak lower," rather than, "Don't yell." Then tell me the logical consequence that is appropriate for my misbehavior.

If you over-react to something I do or do not do, I will probably feel resentful and want to rebel. But if you don't follow your words with actions, I may lose trust and faith in you. Your fairness and consistency really helps me.

Mom/Dad, please learn from books and classes what I am capable of doing and what is normal behavior for my age. It is also important to understand that as a child I probably won't have all of your adult values or interests.

For example, a messy room may not bother me. Teach me how to take care of my things and make my room safe to live in. However, I do need my own space just like you. Please let me be in control of my own room.

As far as chores are concerned, let's sit down together and agree on my responsibilities. An appropriate allowance will reward me for my work and give me the opportunity to learn how to deal with money. Teach me how to save money and allow me to spend the rest as I choose.

Mom/Dad, I do understand that you are human and you may get angry at times. That's okay. Welcome to the human race. However, I would appreciate it if you would deal with your anger constructively. Please accept that you are responsible for all of your feelings, including your anger. You may choose to respond to my misbehavior by being angry. Or you can understand that I may need some guidance, or maybe I am acting out my frustrations, or behaving appropriately for my age. Realize that you always have the choice as to how you respond to me or anyone else.

If you do choose to be angry, please express it by going someplace where you can be alone and yell out your frustrations. You may also want to release your feelings by beating up a soft pillow. Then, when you feel relaxed, ask yourself what you are afraid of. You see, anger is a secondary emotion. Underneath it is a feeling of fear, hurt, or powerlessness.

For example, if I don't do the dishes, you may think that I don't do as you ask, because you are unimportant or disrespected. None of that is true. When you realize that you are important and respected, you will feel calm again. Then please come to me and calmly discuss the problem with the goal of a win-win solution. We both have to feel okay about the solution, because if one of us feels that we lost (that is, not able to live with the agreement) we will feel resentful and in some way get back at the other. That just leads to a negative vicious cycle and we both lose. I am a person just like you. I have feelings and I want to feel heard and powerful too.

By dealing with your anger appropriately and modeling for me win-win problem solving techniques, you are teaching me very important constructive behaviors. These tools will help me greatly when I deal with others. You help me the most when you prepare me for life ~ teach me the values and skills that are necessary for happy and successful living.

One thing that I need you to help me with, to make it in the world, is my self-esteem—how I feel about myself. When I like myself, I believe that I can do many wonderful things and I allow myself to reach my goals. In fact, Mom/Dad, this is the key that opens the door to a very positive, healthy, loving pathway.

If I am misbehaving, hurting people or myself, being abused by others, doing poorly in school, or often sick, it is very likely that my self-esteem is an important underlying cause. These problems are only the tip of the iceberg ~ the symptoms of how I feel about myself. So, please focus on the submerged part of the iceberg, on the causes, and make this question a high priority in your parenting guidelines. How can I help my child believe the truth—that he/she is truly okay, good enough, important, worthwhile, good, lovable, intelligent, attractive, and deserves to be happy, healthy, and successful?

One way you can help me, Mom/Dad, is by believing these things yourself. If you don't, do what you have to do in order to realize your own truths. You may want to read positive books, listen to tapes, or take seminars and workshops. You see, you are also okay. When you believe in yourself, it will be effortless for you to help me own my magnificence. Because then you will be a very positive role model and treat me with unconditional love and I will act accordingly. You will be amazed how many problems (symptoms of our low self-esteem) will disappear when we love ourselves.

Dear Mom/Dad, another way you can help me with my self-esteem is to see me as an individual. I feel devastated when you compare me to anyone else, especially my siblings. I am sure that you expect and want a rose to be just as it is. Nurture and accept me as you would a rose, so that I can grow to be who I am. See all your children as an assortment of beautiful flowers and we will all blossom.

Realize that I have inherited many things from you and I am modeling some of your behavior. But I also have my own unique disposition and lessons to learn. So don't be surprised if in some ways I am very different from you and my siblings.

Also, please be aware of the changing times. It is very likely that the world I am dealing with is very different from the one you experienced. Help me live in the present and focus on my individual needs and wants. Know that sometimes all you can do is offer me information and your opinion. Then tell me that I am responsible for my life and that I will have to deal with the consequences of my behavior. Be patient if I need to struggle through some lessons. Have faith that with your continued love and support, I will be successful.

Mom/Dad, I need your loving actions as well as your words. Smile, be kind, and hug me. I, like everyone else, need at least four hugs a day. Please continue to hug me no matter how old I am. I always need to be hugged.

You may not want to touch me, because you are afraid that it will be sexual. I want you to know that it is very normal to have sexual feelings towards me. After all, you love me and see how beautiful I am. However, please don't act out your sexual feelings with me. That behavior is very inappropriate and will hurt me very much. Find healthy and appropriate outlets for your sexual energy.

Or let a counselor help you constructively deal with your feelings.

Mom / Dad, I am counting on you to protect me from other people using me to act out their sexual needs. Sex is a beautiful, natural, loving act when it is between two consenting, mature people.

When you spend quality time with me, I feel important and worthwhile. Even if you just spend five minutes a day with me, I will treasure those moments. I don't mean watching television together. I am talking about looking into my eyes and interacting with me in a positive way. Some examples are: read to me something appropriate for my age; tell me about your day; or ask me about mine; play with me; or just hug me and tell me you love and appreciate me. Thank you for realizing how important it is to find some time in your busy day when you can be just with me.

Dear Mom / Dad, let me know how you feel, even when you are scared. Sometimes I also feel frightened, as all human beings do, and I need to know that it is okay to feel that way whether I am a boy or a girl. Please don't tell me that I'm a sissy, not a man, or immature. That hurts me deeply because then I feel not okay and frightened for being scared, and I will probably act out my feelings in destructive ways.

For example, if I am scared at school, I may keep getting sick, especially stomach aches (because fear is often expressed in our stomachs), so that I can't go to school. Then I have two problems, illness and fear, and the issue doesn't get resolved. So ask me what I am afraid of and not why I am afraid, so that I don't feel I have to justify my emotions.

Understand that feelings can be irrational, but they are still very real and have to be dealt with constructively. Help me explore my fears and overcome them. I can also learn so much when you tell me how you have overcome your fears. Please don't think that you always have to be strong and perfect. A successful parent acts human, shows their weaknesses as well as their strengths. Actually, it takes a lot of courage to say, "I am scared."

Mom/Dad, if you are not sharing your concerns with me, we may be having problems. For example, if you tell me that I can't do something I want to do, I will probably want to rebel. However, if you tell me that you don't want me to do something, because you are afraid that I will get hurt, I will hear that you care about me and probably honor your request. Or I will reassure you that what I want to do is safe and help you overcome your fear. This is extremely important, especially during the teen years when I am struggling to become my own person.

Please help me grow-up by giving me the freedom I need and I can handle. You can decide that by observing how mature I am and discussing my requests with an open mind. Avoid judging me only by how old I am. You can use my age as a general guideline, but then see me as an individual growing up at my own unique pace.

It hurts me if you try to push me into things I am not ready for, or if you attempt to slow me down. Holding me back because of your own personal fears hurts the two of us. For example, if you are too strict with me because you know what you did at my age and you are afraid that I will be hurt or do the same, I am likely to rebel and purposely do the very things you fear. Or I may decide to let you control me and feel weak and inadequate. Please help me feel strong and confident, so that I can become a healthy, responsible adult.

Dear Mom/Dad, please teach me the facts of life or guide me to appropriate books or classes. Only tell me the information that I asked for. Prepare me for circumstances that I may encounter, because you can't be there to protect me all of the time.

Tell me that you trust that I can take care of myself and that I know right from wrong. That helps me feel good about myself. When I say, "What should I do?" ask me what my choices are. Tell me what options you are aware of and what you might do under the same circumstances. Then make sure that I solve my own problem and realize that I am responsible for my life.

I really do care, Mom/Dad, what you think and feel. I love you and I do want to please you. However, remember that I am here to grow, learn, and follow my own unique path. Help me do that by asking me what I want to do with my life.

It is true that I may have many skills and I am intelligent. But I may not want to pursue some of the things I am capable of. You give me such a gift when you, first of all, reassure me that I don't have to follow in your footsteps or do something just to make you proud of me.

Then ask me, "What excites you? What is your favorite subject or activity?" When I answer, help me explore how I can make a career out of what I enjoy doing. Money doesn't necessarily guarantee me happiness, but doing what I love does.

Dear Mom/Dad, I want you to know how much your relationship with each other affects me. Remember that I make unconscious decisions from my experiences and these beliefs affect my behavior. Therefore, for example, if you two fight, I will probably decide that I am responsible and that I must be a bad person. Especially when I am very young, I think that the world revolves around me and I take responsibility for everything that happens. So if you do argue, please resolve your problem, and be sure to tell me that I am not responsible for your upset and that I am a good person.

By the way, I am also likely to feel responsible for your illness, depression, and even your death. Please teach me that we are all responsible for everything that happens to us ~ that you are responsible for yourself and that I am only responsible for my life.

Mom/Dad, I am observing how you behave and interact with each other in order to learn what is expected of a woman and a man, and the role of a wife and a husband. Therefore, when I grow-up, I will probably act with my spouse as you do with each other.

Your healthy, loving relationship will help me create my own successful marriage. Teach me how to respect, appreciate, and love my partner and myself. Show me how to be warm, caring, and affectionate. Demonstrate how to communicate all my feelings and how to resolve problems. Model for me how to ask for what I want and need. Let me observe how you encourage each other to grow, be your own unique selves, and enjoy each other's differences. Show me how you play and value the time you spend together. Help me understand that the most treasured gift I give my spouse is me, which includes my love, attention, time, and caring. Comfort and material things are nice, but not enough to sustain a healthy relationship.

Mom/Dad, if you don't have a healthy relationship to model, then work towards that goal for yourselves as well as for me. Please avoid turning to me for what you need from each other. I am a child. I can't fill in for your spouse. Expecting me to do that will really hurt me. I will be confused and feel an obligation to you, which is unhealthy and may cause me to be scared of relationships.

I love you both and it hurts me deeply if you tell me negative things about each other. I don't want to be pushed into taking sides. Please don't use me as a weapon to get back at the other ~ that hurts us all. Instead, take your attention off me, face each other, and resolve your differences.

Mom/Dad, it really helps me when you both agree on how to parent me. I need consistency in order to be clear about what is expected of me. However, remember that verbal or physical abuse devastates me and is likely to cause me to feel defeated, rebel, or hurt others. So if one of you is hurting me, I am depending on the other to find a constructive way to protect me. If you don't, I will feel betrayed. I need to feel safe and supported by both of you.

Dear Mom/Dad, it is important for you to have your own interests and do things that you love to do. Making me your sole focus hurts you and me. Yes, it is true that you are a parent, but first of all you are an individual who has needs and wants just like me.

Balance your life by taking care of your responsibilities to others and to yourself. Realize that you are responsible for your own happiness, joy, success, and fulfillment. Then I can model that healthy behavior and not feel guilty for wanting to be my own person. I look forward to when I am around eighteen years old and when you say to me, "I taught you everything that I know.

You are a wonderful, responsible adult and you are free to fly. Go where you want to go, be who you want to be, and remember that I will always love you unconditionally. You don't need a parent anymore telling you what to do; you need a friend. I would like to be one of your best friends."

Mom/Dad, I know that you always do the best that you can at the time. I understand that you have learned many of your parenting skills from your mother and father. And they learned how to parent from their parents and so on, down through the generations. Therefore, if you are having some difficulties with me, it may be because of some parenting patterns that your mother and/or father modeled for you. I have no doubt that they had good intentions and did their best with the information that they had.

Dear Mom/Dad, one way that you can better understand me is to close your eyes, imagine that you are my age and that your parents are standing in front of you. Then tell them what you want and need from them. You will probably find those are the very same things that I need from you.

I know that I have just shared many thoughts with you so I am going to briefly mention a few more and summarize.

As I Grow

Please...

Understand that I am growing up and changing very fast. It may be difficult to keep pace with me, but please try.

Listen to me and give me brief, clear answers to my questions. Then I will want to keep sharing my thoughts and feelings.

Reward me for telling the truth. Then I am not frightened into lying.

Tell me when you make mistakes and what you learn from them. That helps me accept that I am okay, even when I blunder.

Pay attention to me, and spend time with me. That helps me believe that I am important and worthwhile.

Do the things you want me to do. Then I have a good, positive model.

Trust and respect me. Even though I am smaller than you, I have feelings and needs just like you.

Compliment and appreciate me. That will help me feel good, and want to continue to keep my agreements and do nice things for you.

Help me explore my unique interests, talents, and potential. In order for me to be happy, I need to be me, and not you or someone you want me to be.

Be an individual and create your own happiness. That helps me learn how to live a happy, successful, and fulfilling life.

Thank you for hearing me. I love you!

Help Me Grow

Please...

Be consistent with me. Then I can trust your words and actions.

Comfort me when I'm scared, hurt or sad. That will help me feel I'm okay even when I'm not feeling strong or happy.

Take responsibility for all your feelings and actions. That will teach me not to blame others and to take responsibility for my life.

Communicate what you feel hurt or frightened about when you're angry with me. That helps me feel I'm a good person, and learn how to constructively deal with my feelings.

Tell me clearly and specifically what you want. Then it is easier for me to hear you, and I will also know how to communicate my needs in a positive way.

Express to me that I'm okay even when my words or behavior may not be. That will help me learn from my mistakes and have high self-esteem.

Understand and accept me. I may be different than you and I'm okay.

Balance your life between work and play. Then it is easier for me believe that I can grow up, be responsible, and still have fun.

Remember what you wanted when you were my age. Then you'll better understand my needs and interests.

Treat me as an individual. That helps me believe that I can be my unique self.

Hug me and tell me that you care about me. That feels so good, and helps me feel lovable and express caring to others.

Thank you for hearing me. I love you!

As I Grow Up

Please...

Treat me more as a friend and less as a child. That will help me feel like an equal and act more maturely.

Problem-solve with me appropriate boundaries and guidelines. That will help me know you care and I'll be willing to keep our agreements.

Understand that I may need to spend a lot of time with my friends. That will help me learn important social skills with my peers.

Be guided by my level of maturity. Then you will clearly see who I am and make the appropriate decisions.

Realize that times have changed. Then you'll base your opinions on the present and not the past.

Forgive me when I make mistakes. That will help me learn how to forgive myself and others.

Teach me how to be responsible with money. That will help me learn how to be financially independent.

Accept that my values may be different from yours. That will help me feel okay and respect our differences.

Encourage me to keep my room safe, but allow me my private space. That will help me honor your space and privacy.

Remember that I always need your love and support. That will help me feel secure and make the right decisions.

Thank you for preparing me for life. I love you!

As I Break Away

Please...
   Realize that growing-up can be exciting and scary too.
   Be patient if I'm inconsistent.
   Understand that sometimes I may choose to act childish.
   Have faith that I will become more responsible.
   Know that I need to go at my own pace.
   Accept that at times I may want to rebel to feel like an individual.
   Realize that I am influenced by your behavior.
   Understand that I do appreciate your attention and caring.
   Know that unconditional love is your power.
   Help me transform into an independent, mature adult.

Thank you for all your love and support. I love you!

Children Are ....

Gifts from heaven
Here to be their unique selves
Beautiful and sensitive
Wise and talented
A great joy
Basically good and innocent
To be honored and listened to
Reminders for us to play and have fun
Asking for guidance
Creative and adventurous
Deserving of respect and appreciation
Important and worthy of our time and attention
Learning by what they see, hear, and experience.
Flexible and easily influenced
Depending on us to be fair, patient, and understanding
Wanting to be trusted, loved, and accepted
Eagerly waiting to be shown the way
Desiring to feel safe and free
Expressing their need for peace and joy
The foundation for our future

Congratulate yourself for being willing to explore what you can do to be a successful parent. To receive even more insights and solutions, work with the HART exercises in Part III.

Chapter 11

Empowering Communication

*I*n the HART process we view every relationship as three different parts. The analogy is that of a bridge. The two foundations holding up the structure represent each individual's beliefs, self-esteem, values, goals, etc. The third part of the relationship is the bridge itself, which is symbolic of the communication between the two people. Therefore, it takes two individuals with high self-esteem and similar values and goals, as well as good communication, to create a strong bridge or relationship that will withstand whatever happens.

For example, Joe and Lisa loved each other very much, but they had poor communication skills and rated their self-esteems under 5 (with 10 being the highest). This explained why their relationship was rocky. I proposed to the couple that we work on all three parts of their relationship. Joe and Lisa both agreed to see me alone to strengthen their self-esteem and together to improve their communication skills. As a result, they had a 100% chance of enjoying a fulfilling relationship.

However, if the couple had only come into my office together, they would have had one-third of a chance to succeed. Then if only Joe alone was willing to work on his issues privately, their chances would have increased to two-thirds.

It has been a joy to help many couples who were willing to work on all three parts of their relationship and be one of the happy, success stories.

The rest of this chapter will offer you the guidelines for healthy communication so that you can strengthen all your relationships. These include relationships with your loved ones and everyone you come in contact with.

To begin with, it is helpful to accept that we are responsible for our feelings. Getting angry and blaming others for our emotional responses is likely to result in many conflicts and problems.

We can overcome feeling hopeless and helpless when we realize that we only have the power to change ourselves. However, people often respond differently to us when we communicate in more constructive ways. For example, others are more likely to be able to 'hear' our fears rather than our anger. It is also important to share our fears, because they are the emotion that is hidden underneath anger. Therefore, the underlying emotion is fear, and when we are in fear we feel bad.

One useful way to overcome your upsets is a process I call S.O.S. (Morse code for HELP!!) In other words, you are thinking to yourself, "Help, I'm stuck!" The goal of the process is to help you shift from fear to love, so that you can feel good again.

The first thing to do is to ask yourself, "What am I telling myself?" This is a very important question, because it will help you to realize that the cause of your pain is how you interpreted the event that occurred and not the event itself. If you feel bad, you have very likely decided that what happened or did not happen is something negative about you personally. In other words, you have made the event equal to a belief that you are not okay (important, lovable, worthy, good enough, etc.)

The truth is that you are okay no matter what you do and no matter what anyone says or does. Your specific behavior may not be acceptable, but you are okay. For example, being aggressive and hitting someone is not acceptable, but you are basically a good person. (You must be hurting inside if you are hurting someone else or yourself.)

To pull yourself out of your incorrect interpretation of what happened, realize that the 'event' is equal only to the event and that you are okay.

The following is an outline of the S.O.S. Process and two examples:

"What am I telling myself?"
1. "The event = I am not okay."
2. "The event = the event."
3. "I am okay."

Example 1:

1. "I forgot my appointment = I am not okay."
2. "I forgot my appointment = I forgot my appointment."
3. "I am okay."

Example 2:

1. "He didn't call me = I am unimportant."
2. "He didn't call me = He didn't call me."
3. "I am important."

(Note: Instead of yelling at him for not calling, you can now tell him your fear.)

Try this process by filling in your own experience and see if it helps you feel better. If you still feel upset, then you may need to constructively express your emotions. For example, if you are angry you can release your feelings by yelling and hitting a soft pillow. If you are sad, allow yourself to cry. Once you feel calmer, try the S.O.S Process again.

Know that you are worthy, lovable, important, good enough and a good person. Allow yourself to be human, to make mistakes and to learn from them. Communicate with yourself so that you can understand your upsets and overcome them. You deserve to feel good and to have successful relationships.

Are You Listening?

"I should have listened to her. Beverly was trying to tell me how unhappy she was but I wouldn't hear her. Now she is gone and I miss her so much," Allen said, as his body shook with sobs of grief. Allen felt devastated since his wife left him three months ago. He was depressed and losing weight—he had no appetite.

"I'm afraid I'm going to lose my job because I can't concentrate. Getting up in the morning is so difficult. Nothing matters anymore," Allen expressed with despondence. Then he put his head in his hands as he cried some more.

Suddenly he lifted his head up as he yelled out, "Why didn't I listen? I was so stupid! I pride myself in being Allen, the intelligent executive. Allen, the one everyone can rely on to solve problems and to help the company be successful. The truth is that I'm Allen, the big failure. I couldn't make my own marriage succeed. I lost the only woman I have ever loved. I hate myself. I feel so hopeless."

Francine, another client whose marriage also broke up, said with tears in her eyes, "Why didn't I listen to Ron? He tried to talk to me. He wanted to tell me what was bothering him, but I wouldn't take the time to hear him. I made the excuses that I was too busy with dinner, or the children, or had a PTA meeting to go to. What a fool I was. Ron has left me for another woman. I feel so hurt and so angry at myself."

Clyde and Roberta were clients who also learned the hard way about the danger of not listening. They came to see me because their teenage daughter, Lisa, tried to commit suicide. She was still in the hospital recovering from an overdose of drugs. Their doctor had recommended that they see a counselor.

The upset parents shuddered as they related their story to me and admitted that Lisa had tried to tell them numerous times how unhappy she was. Both Clyde and Roberta unfortunately were too busy working, doing chores, or attending charitable organizational meetings to take the time to heed her warnings. They had erroneously made the decision that Lisa was just going through normal teenage growing up problems and thought that these would pass. Clyde and Roberta had learned a very important lesson about listening. They were going to be sure to pay attention to what Lisa and their other children were telling them.

These case studies are just examples of the many clients who did not know how to listen. I shared with them the following helpful hints so that they could really hear what others are telling them.

1. Be clear that you are okay no matter what people say so that you can be objective.
2. Understand that people are responsible (and not you) for how they think and feel.

3. Make an agreement with the other person as to the specific time you will listen to them when you will be rested and alert.
4. Find a quiet place where you will not be distracted.
5. Make sure that you will not be interrupted by phone calls, radio or television programs.
6. Tell them that you really want to hear them and that you appreciate their sharing with you.
7. Clear your mind and be totally present and objective as you listen to what they are trying to tell you.
8. Let them know that you are listening by making eye contact, nodding your head, saying, "Uh huh," or "I hear you."
9. Avoid thinking about what you want to say, being defensive, judging, trying to rescue them, or solving their problems.
10. To make sure that you heard them and they know that you heard them, tell them in your own words, "I heard you say ____."
11 If you need clarity, ask them for more information by saying, "What do you mean?" or "How do you feel?" (Avoid "Why" questions because that word indicates that they have to justify themselves.)
12. Listen to their body language so that you can hear their truth. For example, if their hands are making a fist, they are probably feeling angry even if they deny it.
13. Ask them, "How can I help you?" or "What would you like from me right now?"
14. Reassure them that their feelings are valid even if they seem irrational.
15. Express your compassion and let them know if you feel the same way sometimes.
16. If there are problems to be resolved, ask them if they want you to help them find win-win solutions.
17. Thank them for trusting you and for being willing to share their thoughts and feelings.
18. Schedule another time when you can be there for them.

If you take the time to listen to the people in your life, you can avoid many hardships and you will be greatly rewarded. Enjoy healthy relationships by hearing others and of course, by asking others to listen to you. Be sure that you can say "yes" to the question, "Are you listening?"

The Art of Communication

To begin with you may want to make the following agreement with anyone you wish to communicate with.

"I care about you and I am committed to communicating with you in constructive ways. I realize that I am responsible for all my thoughts and feelings. I am willing to be present and to listen to you. My focus is on accepting both of our viewpoints and creating win-win situations and solutions. It is such a joy to communicate with you and to maintain the bridge between us so that we can be close. I like feeling close to you."

Now that you are clear about your goal, here are some guidelines that can help you keep your communication agreement.

1. Take the time to communicate with yourself. Tune into your own thoughts and feelings to be clear about what you want to share with others.
2. Take responsibility for your thoughts and feelings by beginning your sentences with "I."
3. Ask for what you want instead of telling people what you do not want. For example, "I would like you to calmly tell me what you want," is better than, "Don't yell at me!"
4. Understand that communication is sharing opinions and feelings. Avoid debating, which is the same as trying to prove someone or something right or wrong.
5. Make a statement first so people know what you are thinking. Then ask them for their opinion. For example, "I would like to go to the movie. Would you like to go?"
6. Avoid mind reading. If you are unclear about any communication ask for specifics. For example, "How do you mean that?" "What do you mean?"
7. Watch for non-verbal messages—gestures, posture, tone of voice, etc.—to fully understand what the person is saying.
8. Rather than give advice, point out the different choices you see and allow the other person to make their own decisions.

9. Really listen to what they are trying to tell you. (Avoid thinking about what you want to say next.) Then let them know that you have heard them by repeating what they have said in your own words.
10. To let the other person know that you are listening, use eye contact, or say, "Uh huh" or "I hear you."
11. If a person is not communicating with you, be aware if you are doing one or more of the following: not listening, judging, talking too much, interrupting, not being interested in the other person's communication, being impatient, criticizing, being sarcastic, overreacting, psychoanalyzing, labeling, or cursing.
12. In order to be heard, <u>avoid</u> starting your sentences with the following words, because they often feel like attacks and provoke arguments.

"**I know you** ___." You only know about yourself.

"**I like you, but** ___." The "but" discounts the first part of the sentence.

"**You feel** ___." People do not like to be told how they are feeling.

"**Why are you feeling** ___?" You are asking them to rationally justify their feelings. Emotions are real and valid even if they are irrational.

"**You always or never** ___." These words are too absolute and the listener will be focusing on the times they did or didn't do what they feel they are being accused of so that they can defend themselves.

"**You make me** ___." No one can make you feel a certain way. You are totally responsible for how you perceive things and react to them.

"**Don't you think** ___?" You are implying that they should think your way.

"**You should** ___." These words are telling the other person that they are not okay if they do not do what you say, which often leads to rebellious behavior because they are not feeling that they have a choice.

13. In order to be heard, begin your sentences with the following words:

"I imagine ___." Your imagination is not threatening to another.

"I like you and ___." They are likely to be open to your comment.

"I feel ___." People like to hear what you are feeling.

"What (or How) are you feeling?" These words ask for information and show that you care.

"Sometimes or often ___." People can often handle non-absolutes.

"I resent ___." Taking responsibility for your feelings helps the other person hear you.

"What do you want?" You are helping the other person tell you what they desire. This shows that you care enough to ask.

"I want, prefer or would like ___." People like direct and clear messages.

14. Be aware of your non-verbal messages and be congruent. That is, your body language and words need to be sending the same message. For example, if you say, "What do you want?" with an annoyed tone of voice, you are sending the message that you really do not care about what they want.

15. If you are upset, do what you need to do in order to feel calm so that you can communicate constructively. For example, take a walk, nap, write down your feelings, or yell into a pillow.

16. Create win-win situations by brainstorming until both parties are satisfied with the solution(s). Then work out the specific details so that you can carry out the mutually agreed upon decision(s). These techniques can greatly enhance your relationships. Be forgiving and patient with yourself and others as you acquire the art of communication.

Resentment—the Bite That Holds On

Lindsay gazed at the floor as she gently wiped the tears that were trickling down her wet cheeks. As the forty-two-year-old woman composed herself, she was able to renew eye contact with her husband, Charles, whose eyes were also filled with sadness. They were sitting opposite each other and sharing their long-seated resentments.

Lindsay and Charles did not want a divorce and were committed to improving their relationship. They had also come to the realization that their upsets were affecting their three children.

At our first couple counseling session, they expressed to me the many problems they had been struggling with during most of the twenty-two years of their marriage. Upon further exploration, it was apparent to me that Lindsay and Charles loved each other deeply. They had the same values and similar interests. Each of them had respect for the other and adored their three children.

They were also very active in their community. Since they never argued in public, no one but one close friend knew about their unhappiness. Lindsay and Charles were attractive, well groomed, and financially successful. They were able to fool the community, but not themselves—at least not anymore. Their marriage was in trouble, and the wife and husband could not run away from their reality anymore.

Everything came to a head when their teenage son, Ricky, was having problems in school. Besides not attending classes, Ricky was caught smoking marijuana in the boys' locker room. During their meeting with the principal, he had suggested that Lindsay and Charles seek family counseling.

The principal was wise to know that the children often act out the pain of the family. He understood that even though Ricky was responsible for his actions, the solutions to his problems involved more than himself. The entire unit, his family, needed some resolutions.

When Lindsay and Charles called me for an appointment, I indicated that I wanted them to bring in the entire family for the first session. Once I understood how they reacted to each other and what the problems were, I asked Ricky to come in for a few individual sessions. Then it was time to work with the parents who are the foundation for their family unit.

During the couple counseling session I said, "Lindsay and Charles, resentments are like bites that hold on. They keep you separate and block your love feelings. No matter how spiritual, intelligent, or loving you are, it is important to resolve your resentments so that you can be close."

I told them that they were unique, but their problems were not. In the course of counseling many couples, I found that the lack of love was rarely the problem. However, hidden resentments caused many bad feelings and covert or overt conflicts.

Both Lindsay and Charles had a tendency to withhold their upsets. Therefore, their home atmosphere was relatively quiet, with only infrequent outbursts of anger that were not long-lasting. However, there were lots of covert expressions of anger by way of withdrawal of affection, avoidance of each other, and subtle sarcasm.

Because Lindsay and Charles avoided expressing their feelings, their relationship had become more like roommates than an intimate couple. Their children, to their surprise, were subconsciously sensitive to the negative undercurrent and were feeling upset. Typical of young people, although it is totally illogical, they subconsciously felt responsible for their parents' pain.

At this point, Charles and Lindsay began to understand how their unfinished business with each other was affecting their marriage and their family. Scared but highly motivated, they were willing to do a clearing process. I first suggested to them that they tell each other the following, "I love you and I never meant to hurt you. I also understand that you never purposely did anything to cause me pain. I want to be close to you. Therefore, I'm going to share my resentments with you so that I can release them. Please just listen to my upsets. Let's learn from our mistakes and forgive each other."

After Charles and Lindsay repeated those healing words, they felt ready to unload their hidden "baggage." I asked Lindsay to express a specific resentment in one sentence by beginning with the words, "I feel resentful when you ____." Then I asked Charles to repeat back what he heard in his own words. If Lindsay felt satisfied that Charles had listened and understood her resentment, we switched roles, and Charles went on to share his resentment.

Both Charles and Lindsay felt sad as they were reliving those painful times. They were surprised to hear about incidents that had happened early in their marriage, over twenty years ago. They were even more amazed when they realized how those upsets were still affecting them in the present.

Releasing their resentments in this constructive way helped them to feel a great sense of relief. The "bite" was finally letting go. The unfinished business from the past, that was keeping them separate, was finally being removed.

At the end of the session, Charles and Lindsay admitted that they were feeling vulnerable, but also much closer to each other. They rose from their chairs, smiled, and lovingly hugged each other. The couple knew that they had more work to do, but they were confident that they were on their way to having the fulfilling relationship they deeply desired.

Win-Win Problem Solving

I have discovered that most of my clients' problems were unresolved for a very long period of time. Many individuals had been suffering for over twenty years with the same issue. Often couples were fighting repeatedly over the identical problem for at least thirty years or most of their married life.

How unfortunate it is that we are not taught how to communicate or how to resolve our issues. I would love to see required Communication and Problem Solving classes in all schools, from the first grade up. I believe that they could make a very positive impact on our society, and help to prevent and resolve many of our problems.

Being human, it is normal and expected to have problems. The healthy person and couple are not free of problems. However, they are successful, because they know how to identify their issues and how to resolve them.

The following guidelines can help you solve your problems so that you can function in a healthier way and learn from your conflicts, and be in harmony with yourself and others.

1. Understand that you can only solve problems when you are in your logical mode (left brain).
2. Begin by expressing all of your emotions by yourself in a constructive way. For example, if you are angry, you can release your feelings by writing them down, yelling and hitting a soft pillow, taking a walk, or listening to relaxing music.

3. When you feel calm and clear about the problem, write it down as a question. For example, "How can I have enough time for myself?"

4. Then write down all of the possible answers to your question. Let your creativity and sense of humor help you. Sometimes the most outrageous ideas become the best solutions. You may even want to ask a friend to assist you. Some examples are: get up earlier, limit my organizational commitments, plan at least two evenings at home, fill in my alone time in my appointment book before I schedule anything else, plan a week-end away every month and say "no" to people without feeling guilty.

5. Now cross off any ideas that you are not willing to accept. Be honest and patient with yourself. You may find that you can only change one or two things at a time, especially if you have been struggling with this issue for a while.

6. Look at the remaining solutions and work out the specific details necessary to carry them out. For example, decide which outside commitments you need to let go of and who you need to say "no" to. Then plan when and how you will address these people.

7. In order to help you change your behavior patterns, it can be helpful to close your eyes and to visualize yourself spending more time alone and doing what you want to do.

8. Writing positive thoughts can help you affirm your new patterns. Continue to write, say, sing, or read them until you have integrated your new belief or pattern. Some examples are: "I, (your name), am spending more time by myself and people accept me. I, (your name), am saying 'no' to other people and I am okay. I, (your name), realize that I need more alone time so that I can rest and rejuvenate, which is a gift to myself and others."

9. Reward yourself for being willing to solve your problem. You deserve it!

In order to solve a conflict with another person, follow the same outline. Be sure that you do not make comments to each other during the brainstorming (#4), so that your creativity will not be stifled. It is also important not to react in any way if either one of you crosses off an idea (#5) that you do not like. Remember that you both have to be able to live with the solutions in order for them to work. Strive only for win-win solutions and you will be successful.

If you do not come to an acceptable agreement or you still feel upset with yourself or another, then you have probably not worked on the real issue. Explore the actual problem and then begin the process again.

This technique can be used successfully with anyone, including your family members, friends, managers, fellow employees, and neighbors.

As we solve our issues with ourselves and with the people in our lives, we can be happier, healthier, and more successful. When we can solve our conflicts with win-win solutions with other countries, what a peaceful world this will be.

Chapter 12

Releasing Anger

*M*any people are joyously singing: "Let there be peace on earth and let it begin with me." I love that song, and I totally believe in what it is telling us. I am convinced that when we human beings, who inhabit this world, experience inner peace, then and only then, will we actualize long-lasting world peace.

I used to feel so powerless when I read the horrible stories in the newspapers. Then I realized that by focusing on transforming and healing myself and by helping others do the same, I had the power to make a difference in the world. I became aware of the inner turmoil within myself and others, which prevents us from feeling peacefully powerful. I kept exploring what we need to do in order to end our internal wars and to experience inner peace. I discovered that one important thing we have to learn is how to deal with our personal anger. This common feeling is often denied, misunderstood, and misused. It is dangerous for us and the world when we don't constructively express this normal human emotion. The following is what I have learned about dealing with anger.

1. *What is anger?*
    Anger is a normal, healthy human emotion. Whenever you are experiencing anger, you are also feeling fear, hurt, and/or powerlessness. Therefore, when you deal with your anger, you also need to deal with all the underlying emotions.

2. *Where in your body do you feel anger?*
   Most people feel anger in the form of tension or pain in their forehead, jaw, cheeks, temples, arms, hands, center of the back of the neck, and the back (especially the shoulder blades and the lower back).

3. *What are some physical problems or illnesses that may result from suppressed anger?*
   Some physical problems that may indicate that anger is present are: headaches; jaw, gum, and teeth problems (from grinding the teeth); arthritis in the fingers or hands; back problems; stroke and heart attack ("I am busting a gut"); high blood pressure ("I am boiling"); bursitis in the shoulder ("I want to hit someone"); constipation; and extreme tiredness.

   (Note: depression is anger turned inwards. When you release your anger in a constructive way, your depression is also likely to be released.)

4. *Is anger a good (positive) or bad (negative) emotion?*
   Anger is one of many emotions (feelings). Emotions are not good or bad. They are feelings that have to be expressed. People have the choice of dealing with anger in a positive or negative way (constructively or destructively).

5. *How do people express anger in a negative way?*
   Some people act out their anger in what is called Active Aggression. Others act it out in Passive Aggression. And some people alternate between active and passive aggression.

   Active Aggressors may shout, curse, or physically attack a person or a thing. Some examples are: hitting, rape, murder, starting fires, and defacing property.

   Passive Aggressors may quietly withdraw, be late, be sarcastic, procrastinate, forget important dates, verbally attack with a soft voice and a smile, or overeat.

6. *Does physical activity help release anger?*
   Physical activity helps relieve some of the angry energy that results from angry feelings, but it does not *resolve* the anger. Therefore, the angry feelings still present will create more angry energy,, and you have to keep running faster or hitting the ball harder in order to keep from exploding.

7. *Why do most people deny or resist accepting their angry feelings?*
Most people block their anger because they are afraid that if they are angry they will:

a) hurt someone else or themselves
b) be hurt by someone else
c) be out of control or crazy
d) be wasting their time ("I don't accomplish anything, so why bother?)
e) be bad or not O.K.
f) be unladylike
g) be rejected
h) be like their parent and they hated it when their parent was angry
i) be too powerful
j) be giving their power to the other person ("The other person will know they won or got to me.")

8. *How can I deal with my anger in a positive way?*
You can deal with your anger in a constructive way by first acknowledging it. Then by yourself or with someone you trust, angrily yell and hit a soft pillow until your anger is released. After that, get in touch with an underlying feeling, which may be fear, hurt, or powerlessness. Once you have owned and expressed all your feelings, you are ready to make an affirmation (a positive thought). For example:

a) If you are angry when "J" comes home late, release your feelings by hitting a soft pillow, as you say "I'm angry at you 'J' for being late. I'm angry!" (Continue to yell until you feel relaxed.)
b) Then say to yourself, "When you are late, I'm scared that I'm unimportant."
c) Affirmation: "I'm beginning to believe that I'm important."
d) If you are feeling calm, because you understand all your feelings and have released them, decide if you need or want to talk to the person about the issue of coming late—in person, by letter, or by phone.
e) Finally, compliment yourself for dealing with your anger in a healthy, positive, and constructive way.

Chapter 13

Intuitive Problem Solving

"What am I to do?" Do you have a tendency to feel stressed when you think about all the possibilities? Once you have finally made a decision, do you then wonder if you made the right choice?

If you are like me, you weigh everything, see both sides and find it difficult to make decisions. For my sanity and reduction of stress, that causes dis-ease, I fortunately discovered a better way. I call it Intuitive Problem Solving.

Everyone is intuitive and has the ability to tap into this 24 hours a day, seven days a week, year round (even on holidays) free consultation.

Intuition is the wise part of us that has all of our answers. How convenient it is to innately have this valuable resource.

The following are four other ways to connect with this "wise service". Everyone has at least one dominant method and a secondary one. See if you can identify your particular intuitive strengths.

If you are <u>clairvoyant</u>, you are visual or "see" things or people in your mind's eye (third eye in the center of your forehead).

To be <u>clairaudient</u> means that you hear things that are not on the physical plane.

You are <u>clairsentient</u> if you have a gut feeling of something being appropriate or not.

Finally, you are <u>telepathic</u> if you have a knowing of something.

No matter which mode you have of receiving your intuitive messages, they are all equally valid. Your intuition offers you very important information. There are many stories of people's lives being saved, as well as problems prevented or solved, because they listened to and acted on their intuition.

If it is so valuable, why do so many people disown this part of them? Our society mainly values our thinking minds, which is the left part of the brain and requires physical, logical proof. Intuition is in the right part of the brain and is metaphysical— beyond the physical. Like feelings, it is not based on logic. Therefore, it can be more difficult to accept. However, that does not mean that it is any less valuable.

In fact, intuition is wiser than the mind. This is because the mind only knows what it has learned and bases its information on the basic five senses. Wisdom comes from beyond thoughts and physical perceptions. You can give people information, but you cannot teach wisdom, which comes from an inner source— your intuition.

You can learn how to listen to your inner messages and tap into your wisdom. There are many ways to do that. However, they have some common guidelines.

The first important process is to overcome any fears you have of the situation. For example, if you want to purchase a house you may be concerned that it is the only house you will be happy in. You can let go of that limiting belief by saying, "I release the fear that this is the only right house for me." Follow that with, "I trust that if this house is right for me, I will be able to purchase it. Otherwise there will be another one which is better for me."

Then it is helpful to let go of any attachments your mind or emotions may have to the house by saying, "I am not attached to the answer. I know and trust that the perfect house is available to me at the perfect time."

The next step is to close your eyes and take a few deep breaths. Then tap into your intuitive messages by asking, "Is it for my highest good to purchase this house now?" Once you receive your answer, have the courage to act on it.

If I have a decision to make, I often wait until the morning when I first awaken to check in with my intuition. That is because my logical mind has not "kicked in" yet because I am still in that semi-conscious state. However, I also connect with my intuition throughout the day.

If I need to make an important decision, I will check in with my intuition for a few days. If I am facing a crucial issue, I am likely to contact an intuitive friend who has no emotional charge on the issue for a more objective answer. It is even fun to get a few intuitive opinions to see what happens.

Another way I connect with my inner wisdom is through kinesiology—muscle testing. The general rule here is that a strong muscle means "yes" and a weak one means "no". For example, you can have someone try to push your outstretched arm down as you say a question out loud.

I also pay attention to the center of my chest as I ask my question. If my chest feels tight, I know that it is a negative answer. An expansion tells me "yes".

Finally, I do the Wise Person Process (Note Chapter 21) as another way to tap into my inner wisdom.

The more you practice listening to your intuition, the easier it becomes. Have fun with it. For example, when I awaken in the morning, I guess what time it is before I open my eyes. When the telephone rings, I sometimes tune into my intuition to find out who is calling.

I suggest that you value and trust your inner wisdom, no matter what other people say or do. Choose an easier way to resolve your problems. Choose your intuition.

Chapter 14

Overcoming Addictions

*W*hen we are addicted to someone or something, it means we behave like a slave because we allow the strong habit to control us. It is what we do in excess in order to avoid feeling our painful feelings (hurt, anger, fear, loneliness, emptiness, etc.). Therefore, addictions are often the *symptoms* and *not the causes* of our troubles. They make us feel better for a short period of time but then we soon need another "fix", because we still have the pain from the underlying negative feelings.

Ironically, our addictions cause us even more problems and result in additional pain. For example, an alcoholic often loses his or her job, has unsuccessful relationships and suffers from physical problems brought on by the alcohol. The workaholic finds their loved ones complaining that they are never around. They may make more money but probably spend more for medical problems because of their self-induced stress.

The first helpful thing to do to overcome your addictions is to be honest with yourself and recognize your extreme behaviors. The following questionnaire will help you to identify your unhealthy habits.

Put a <u>check</u> next to the description of your behavior.

A. I eat or drink in excess:

___1. Food
___2. Alcohol

___3. Coffee
___4. Carbonated beverages
___5. Chocolate
___6. Ice cream
___7. Candy
___8. Pastry
___9. Bread
___10. Other _____

B. I feel a compulsion (not in control of myself) to do a lot of:

___1. Work
___2. Running/Sports
___3. Shopping
___4. Yelling
___5. Creating
___6. Smoking
___7. Gambling
___8. Drugs
___9. Cleaning/organizing
___10. Other _____

C. I feel no matter how much I have, I always want more:

___1. Money
___2. Sex
___3. Affection
___4. Cars
___5. Clothes
___6. Material things
___7. Attention
___8. Machines/Tools (including computers)
___9. Power
___10. Other _____

D. I spend a lot of time:

___1. Playing
___2. Reading
___3. Writing

___4. Watching television/movies
___5. Collecting things
___6. At the computer
___7. Complaining
___8. Fixing things
___9. Joking
___10. Other ____

To further understand yourself, fill in the following statements:

E. When I am upset I:

1. _____

2. _____

3. _____

F. I have a habit of:

1. _____

2. _____

3. _____

G. I am addicted to:

1. _____

2. _____

3. _____

H. I wish that I could stop (a behavior):

1. _____

2. _____

3. _____

Positive Behavior

Now that you understand your avoidance habits, write a check next to the following things that appeal to you to help you overcome your addictions.

When I am aware of my habit controlling me, I can do the following:

1. Take at least ten slow, deep breaths (count to six on the inhale and exhale).
2. Ask myself, "What negative thought am I thinking?" Then imagine that
3. I am burning it away and replacing it with a positive thought.
4. Listen to a self-help tape.
5. Read a self-help book.
6. Drink water with or without lemon.
7. Eat a low calorie vegetable.
8. Take a walk.
9. Call someone I trust and share my feelings with them.
10. Take a class to raise my self-esteem.
11. Join a support group or start my own.
12. Work with a professional counselor on my underlying issues.
13. Do something healthy to nurture myself.
14. Deal with my feelings in a constructive way.
15. Work with other exercises in this book.
16. Take classes or read books on communication.
17. Do something fun (examples: dance, sing, play music).
18. Improve my parenting skills.
19. Learn more about how to have successful relationships.
20. Realize who I learned my habit from (examples: parents, friends, lovers). Notice what it did to them and decide if I still want to continue to do that extreme behavior.
21. Focus on balancing my life between work and play.
22. Read some inspiring poems or literature.
23. Other _____.

Now make a plan of action to overcome your addictions and take control of your life. Congratulate yourself, be patient and take one day at a time.

Chapter 15

Balancing Your Life

*I*n order to be a whole person, feel good and avoid burnout, we need to balance our lives. Basically, we have four parts: physical, mental, emotional and spiritual. All of our parts are important and valuable. They all need acceptance, appreciation and time to be expressed. The following outline can help you balance your life:

1. First, look at your year. What are your goals in each area of your life? (Goals need to be specific, measurable, attainable, and truly things you desire.)

    Fill in your answers.
    A) My relationship or social goals are _____.
    B) My professional goals are _____.
    C) My financial goals are _____.
    D) My vacation goals are _____.
    E) My physical body goals are _____.
    F) My mental goals are _____.
    G) My emotional goals are _____.
    H) My spiritual goals are _____.
    I) My family goals are _____.
    J) My goals to have fun and play are _____.

2. Now in a monthly calendar, set your goal to balance your life and begin to schedule your months.

Examples: a weekend a month to go away, one day of each week to have alone time, specific working hours, days off, classes and responsibilities.

3. Look at the whole picture? Does it look balanced?

4. Then, in a weekly calendar, schedule and balance your week.

5. Finally, have a daily calendar and look at your day. Notice if it is balanced. Have you included all your parts (physical, mental, emotional and spiritual)?

    Examples: Ask yourself, "When Am I: working, playing, exercising, eating, resting, socializing, spending alone time and saying my affirmations.

    Congratulate yourself for balancing your life!

Chapter 16

Career Guidance

Studies have shown that men and women, who are millionaires, all had in common the fact that they loved what they did. I believe that they also were a lot happier and more fulfilled than those who did not follow their heart, unique gifts, or interests.

It was such a joy to meet people who loved their jobs or professions. Unfortunately, that has not often been the case. I find that most people do what they can to earn the most money or please their parent(s).

Barry, a 32-year-old computer salesman, came to me because he was very frustrated. He was doing well in his job but was not very happy. However, he did not know what else he wanted to do. His Dad had wanted him to follow in his footsteps and so he did.

In the course of our counseling sessions, Barry realized that he had a gift of helping people laugh and feel better. He explored massage therapy and loved it. When I saw him a year later at a luncheon, I hardly recognized him. Barry had exchanged his suit for some casual clothing and he looked very happy.

Are you doing what you love? Do you feel that you are expressing your unique gifts, strengths, or talents?

The following exercise can assist you to clarify what you would love to be doing.

Career Exercise

1. If I could do anything I wanted to in the form of work or service, I would ____ (finish the sentence).
2. If I followed my heart and my joy, I would ____.
3. My gifts, strengths and talents include ____.
4. I enjoy (or enjoyed) when I ____.

When you feel clear about what you choose to do, find the courage to follow your dream. If you are need assistance to overcome your fears of being who you truly are, then I suggest that you work with the HART exercises in Part III.

Part III

Transformation:
H A R T Exercises

Chapter 17

Affirmations: The Power of Positive Thinking

*B*efore we begin the HART exercises, it is helpful to understand how to make affirmations.

Our thoughts are magnetic—they attract to us whatever we are thinking. Positive thinking creates positive results. Negative thoughts attract negative experiences and keep us stuck. Many of our fear-based beliefs came from decisions we made from our past experiences.

For example, if you feel guilty about something you did, you may decide that you are bad and that you don't deserve to be prosperous.

In order to move on in your life and enjoy more love, health and abundance, it is necessary to release negative self-defeating thoughts and replace them with positive ones. These are called affirmations.

You can easily change any negative thought into a positive one. Listen to your daily thoughts and conversations. Whenever you hear a negative thought say, "cancel," or imagine that you are erasing it. You can also imagine that you are burning it away with a laser beam, or whatever image works for you. Then change it to a positive one. After awhile, you will begin to do it automatically.

You can also become aware of your negative thoughts by making a list of them. Write at the top of a piece of paper, I am afraid that ___ and fill in the blank with whatever negative thoughts come to mind. Choose one and change it to a positive thought. Start with the word, "I," followed by your name and the new thought.

For example: The negative thought or fear, I am afraid that I don't deserve money, can be changed to: I, (your name), deserve an abundance of money.

Since many of our thoughts come from comments we heard from others, it is helpful to also substitute, "You" and "S/he" for "I." For example: You, (your name), deserve an abundance of money. S/he, (your name), deserves an abundance of money.

It is important to be honest with yourself and feel okay wherever you are at the time. Therefore, if you are having difficulty accepting your affirmation, you can add some words to make it more believable. For example: I, (your name), am *beginning to believe* that I deserve *some* money. After awhile, you are likely to change it to: I, (your name), am *beginning to believe* that I deserve an abundance of money. And finally to: I, (your name), deserve an abundance of money.

If you still don't believe the new affirmation, then write your negative thought on a piece of paper. Follow it by the word "because" and list the reasons. For example: I, (your name), don't deserve an abundance of money because: I stole a dollar from my father when I was a child. I don't know how to handle money. I am afraid it will make me greedy for more. I'm worthless.

Now, on another piece of paper, write an affirmation for each negative belief. Some examples are: I, (your name), forgive myself for taking a dollar from my father when I was a child. I, (your name), am beginning to believe that I know how to handle money. I, (your name), believe that I can have money and be generous. I, (your name), am a worthwhile person.

Now throw away the negative thoughts and say the positive ones.

If you're still not convinced, you can do the following exercise. Write your affirmation on the left hand side of a piece of paper and your feelings on the right. Continue to do this until you are finally ready to accept your affirmation. Some examples are:

I, (your name), deserve money. No, I don't.

I, (your name), deserve money. No way!

I, (your name), deserve money. Why?
I, (your name), deserve money. Why not?
I, (your name), deserve money. Well, maybe.
I, (your name), deserve money. Well, maybe a little.
I, (your name), deserve money. Yes, I do deserve money.

If this doesn't help and you find yourself getting increasingly more negative, you probably have to go a little deeper. Perhaps there is another negative thought underneath the one you've been working on.

For example: Behind the belief I don't deserve money could be the belief that money is evil. A possible affirmation is: I, (your name), am beginning to believe that money is one way I express caring to myself and others.

If you were not able to find any other negative thoughts, ask yourself what you're getting out of holding onto the belief that you don't deserve money. Chances are that you are staying safe. The affirmation can be:

I, (your name), have an abundance of money and I am safe.

The following are several more suggestions for writing affirmations:

1. Keep them short.
2. Use only positive words. For example, write I am good instead of I am not bad.
3. Stay in the present. Avoid statements like, I will or I hope to. Instead, write, I am.
4. Focus on only a few affirmations at a time.
5. Say your affirmations several times with feeling (as if it is already happening in your life), record them on tape and play them back, or sing them out loud. Repetition is important—review them often until they become part of your automatic thinking.
6. Write an affirmation on a card and place it where you will see it often. Example: refrigerator door, bathroom mirror, bedside table, or desk.

When you choose to be conscious of what you are thinking and saying, remove negative thoughts and replace them with positive ones, you will have the power to easily draw to you what you desire. You do deserve love, health, happiness and success in every area of your life.

It is important to remember to always eliminate the negative thought before you make a positive one—just like you remove old clothes from your draw to make room for the new.

Now you are ready to proceed with the rest of the chapters. The empowering exercises can assist you to succeed in many areas of your life. You can work with them in order, or go to the ones that you feel drawn to. It is helpful to write your answers in a notebook so that you can repeat the exercises, continue to heal yourself, and create what you want in your life. Enjoy the process!

Chapter 18

Twenty Blocks to Prosperity

*I*ssues around money are very common. I once sat down and typed all the fears I heard my clients uncover when I was assisting them in the HART process. I was surprised to see how many there were. No wonder there are so many people struggling with money.

The following is a list of negative beliefs that are associated with money that can sabotage your prosperity. You may want to put a <u>check</u> next to the ones you relate to.

   1. Money is evil.
   2. Wealthy people are materialistic, superficial snobs.
   3. Rich people are mean and dishonest.
   4. It is not safe to be prosperous.
   5. Money is scarce.
   6. Money means responsibility.
   7. You have to struggle to get money.
   8. Prosperity does not fit my self-image.
   9. I can't be more prosperous than my parents.
  10. I won't be prosperous because I am angry with my parents.
  11. If I make a lot of money I will not have time for my family or myself.
  12. If I am prosperous people will reject me.
  13. If I have an abundance of money people will want to be with me only for my money.

___14. I don't deserve prosperity.

___15. I feel guilty for having more than others.

___16. If I have money I will have to take care of others.

___17. If I am prosperous I can't be spiritual.

___18. If I have an abundance of money I will have to pay a lot of taxes.

___19. If I am prosperous my personality will change.

___20. Money can control me.

Recognizing and overcoming your fears of abundance will help you create the prosperity you desire. If you related to any of the negative statements, I suggest that you work through the issue(s) in the exercises in Chapter 20, "Allowing Yourself to Succeed."

Chapter 19

Dare To Be Slim

Overweight has become a serious problem. The extra pounds often affect peoples' health and self-esteem

The following is a summary and examples of the unconscious fears I discovered that sabotage people from being their desired weight. I believe that these negative thoughts, based on negative experiences, are some of the major causes of weight problems. You may want to put a check next to the ones you identify with.

___1. If I am slim and attractive, people will reject me. (Peers were jealous of her attractiveness when she was developing.)

___2. It is not safe to be slim. (She was molested when she was thin.)

___3. If I am slim I will attract another relationship and I am afraid to be vulnerable and get hurt again. (She was hurt in a previous relationship so she built a wall of fat.)

___4. If I am slim, I will be sick. (He was thin and sick as a child.)

___5. If I am slim, I will be weak. (When he was a thin boy, a bully attacked him.)

___6. I overeat because I am afraid that I won't have enough food later. (He often went hungry when he was growing up.)

___7. I can't handle all the attention I get from men when I am slim. (She feels embarrassed when men compliment her body with whistles, looks, or compliments.)

___8. I am afraid that men will only want me for my body. (She wants to also be appreciated for her intelligence.)

___9. Food means to me love and attention. (As he was growing up, he only felt loved when he was eating food.)

___10. I am afraid to feel my feelings. (She stuffed her fears and anger.)

___11. I am angry with my parent and spouse for being so critical. (They want her to be thin and she overeats for revenge.)

___12. I don't deserve to be slim and attractive. (She feels guilty for hurting her sibling.)

___13. I don't want to be tempted to have an affair. (Men are attracted to her when she is slim.)

___14. Being slim does not fit my self-image. (She was always overweight.)

___15. I don't know what my life would be like if I was slim. (She had a fear of the unknown.)

If you related to any of the fears mentioned above, I suggest that you work with the HART exercises in the next chapter. Once you overcome your blocks to being your desired weight, you are more likely to exercise regularly, eat healthy foods and drink liquids that support your goal. Know that you can win the "battle of the bulge."

Chapter 20

Allowing Yourself to Succeed

The following exercises can help you reach your personal and professional goals. Some of them are creative visualizations where you will close your eyes and see or sense images. In other processes you can write your responses on paper, or on a computer.

You have all the answers inside of you. These exercises are designed to help you get in touch with your internal wisdom, and identify and overcome any negative issues in your subconscious—your blocks to success and happiness.

You may find it useful to repeat some of the processes, so that you can release even more blocks to your success. Remember that you are very powerful and that you can create what you want in your life. You are here to be happy and successful and you deserve it all. Go for it!

Grounding Cord Process

After you do a visualization process, you may feel spacey. It is helpful to eat something that grows in the ground, or hug a person, or a tree. You can also do the following exercise.

Close your eyes and imagine or sense that there are grounding cords going down from the soles of your feet to the center of the earth. There are two plates there with your name on them. Connect the grounding cords to the plates and feel grounded. Take two deep breaths and slowly open your eyes.

Safe Place Process

The following exercise can help you feel relaxed and safe so that you can deal with your issues. It is also a wonderful meditation that can assist you to calm your mind and feel good.

Close your eyes and take two deep breaths.
Allow yourself to be aware of your body and notice if you have any tension anywhere. If you do, tell that part to relax.
Now imagine or sense a place where you feel safe. It could be a beach, forest, meadow, mountaintop, or your own bedroom, or living room. Imagine any place where you feel safe, and be there now.
Where are you? What are you seeing? What are you hearing?
How are you feeling?
Now imagine a color that represents calmness and safety to you. Imagine that color is coming into your lungs as you inhale and flowing throughout your entire body, bringing you a deeper level of calmness and safety.
Know that whenever you choose to, you can return to your safe place and breathe in your calming color.
Do the Grounding Cord process and take two deep breaths.

Wise Person Process

This exercise can assist you to connect with your wise person in your "attic", so that you can receive guidance and answers to your questions. The wise person image appears in many forms. Some examples are: your higher self, old Father Time, or a brilliant white light

Close your eyes and take two deep breaths.
Imagine that you are in your safe place (note previous exercise).
Now allow yourself to see or sense your wise person who is all-good, all-knowing, and surrounded by white light, coming towards you.
As your wise person is getting closer, allow yourself to see the image more clearly. What are you seeing?

Do you trust your wise person? If you don't, allow another wise person to come to you who you do trust to give you sound answers.

Allow yourself to ask your wise person any question you want to ask about success (relationships, prosperity, weight, etc.).

What is your wise person telling you?

Your wise person has a gift for you. Allow yourself to receive the gift. What are you receiving? What does your gift mean to you?

You may want to thank your wise person for the wisdom and the gift.

Know that you can always connect with your wise person (your inner wisdom) to answer your questions.

Do the Grounding Cord process and take two deep breaths.

The following exercises can help you overcome many blocks to success:

Overcoming Fears

This empowering process will help you become aware of negative beliefs that are keeping you stuck. Then you will change them to positive ones and allow yourself to have what you desire. It is important to set a specific goal that is all positive, measurable, in the present and what you truly desire.

1) Choose one goal you wish to focus on. For example:
   I am earning $75,000 plus this year.
   I am a manager.
   I am in a fulfilling relationship.
   I am healthy.

2) Now write down your goal on a piece of paper.

3) Now write: *I can't* _____ (fill in your goal), because _____. Example:
   I can't earn $75,000 plus this year, because *I am lazy.*

4) Keep reading or saying these words and write down whatever comes to your mind. More examples:
   I don't deserve it.
   I am not smart enough.
   It is too hard.

5) When you feel complete with this process and you have no other thoughts, then write: I *won't* _____ (fill in your goal), because _____. Example:
   I won't earn $75,000 plus this year, because *I'll be too busy and I won't have enough time to spend with my family.*

6) Keep reading or saying these words and writing down whatever comes to your mind. More examples:
   I will have to pay too much money for taxes.
   People will want me to take care of them.
   My father will be happy and I am angry at him.
   No man will want me.

7) On a second piece of paper, write the words, My Affirmations, and then:
   I *am* _____ (fill in your goal), because _____.

8) Now read each negative thought (*can't* and *won't* statements) and write a positive thought for each one. (Note the chapter, "Affirmations: The Power of Positive Thinking"). Fill in your name. Examples:
   I, _____, *am smart enough.*
   I, _____, *am capable.*
   I, _____, *deserve it.*
   I, _____, *have enough money for taxes and myself.*
   I, _____, *can say "no" to others and I am okay.*
   I, _____, *choose to make myself happy.*
   I, _____, *am ambitious.*

9) Then throw away, or burn in a fireplace the sheet(s) with the negative thoughts as you say, "I am letting go of my fears". (Notice if you feel lighter.)

10) Save the sheet of paper with the affirmations. Say, sing, or write them daily until they are a part of your automatic thinking.

Success Means

As I discussed earlier, because many people have a fear that success has a scary consequence, they push away what they desire. It is helpful to get in touch with the fear and release it. You can also replace the word "success" with your specific goal. For example: being slim, a fulfilling relationship, prosperity, or a promotion.

Say or write: Success means to me _____ and finish the sentence with a negative thought. Then change it to a positive one. Repeat this process until you feel complete. For example:

> *Success means to me I won't have enough time for myself.*
> *I, _____ am successful, and I have enough time for myself.*

Self-image

It is important to update how you see yourself. If you were unsuccessful in the past, you may not be able to imagine yourself any differently. This exercise can help you change your negative self-image to a positive one.

1. Close your eyes and take two deep breaths.
2. Now allow yourself to visualize or sense your old self-image. How do you look?
3. Allow yourself to imagine to the right of your inner screen your new self-image. How do you look?
4. Now imagine that you are your new self-image. How are you feeling?
5. If you are ready to let go of the old self-image, then thank the old one for serving you and imagine it is leaving.
6. Now imagine how your life is different with your new self-image.
7. Do the Grounding Cord process and take two deep breaths.

Forgiveness of Others

Sometimes we sabotage our success because we are trying to get back at others. Our resentments and anger hurt us. It is helpful to release these negative feelings in a healthy way and forgive people for their words or actions that did not feel good. (Remember that what people say or do is about them and not you. You are okay no matter what people say or do.)

1. Take the time to be in a safe place where you will feel free to express your angry feelings at another person. Remove any jewelry and put a soft pillow in front of you. Say the words, "I am angry with you for ___" and finish the sentence. Make a fist and hit the pillow. Be real with your feelings by yelling or expressing them in an angry tone. (Raise your voice from your abdomen and not from your throat to avoid hurting it.) Continue to do that until you feel better.
2. Write an affirmation. Examples:
   I, _____, forgive Dad for yelling at me.
   I, _____, accept that Dad was yelling at me because he was scared.
   I, _____, have compassion for Dad's pain and I forgive him.
   I, _____, am okay and good enough no matter what anyone says or does.

I Deserve Success

Everyone deserves success (healthy bodies and relationships, prosperity, fulfilling careers, desired weight, etc.). It is our birthright. This process can help you to reach your personal and professional goals.

1. Write down on a piece of paper: I don't deserve success because _____ and write down whatever comes up. Continue saying these words and writing down your responses until you have no other thoughts. Examples:
   I am not a good person.
   I make mistakes.
   I am jealous of others who are successful.

2.   Now change the negative thoughts to positive ones. Fill in your name. Examples:

I, _____, *am a good person*

I, _____, *learn from my mistakes.*

I, _____, *am happy for others who are successful.*

3.   Now say, sing, or write your affirmations daily until they are a part of your automatic thinking.

Self-Forgiveness

When we feel we did something wrong, we often feel guilty and punish ourselves in some way. We often do this by not allowing ourselves to have what we desire. It is important for us to learn from the experience and forgive ourselves, so that we can actualize our goals.

1.   Take the time to be in a safe place where you will feel free to express your angry feelings at yourself. Remove any jewelry and put a soft pillow in front of you. Say the words, "I am angry with you for _____ (and finish the sentence)." Make a fist and hit the pillow. Be real with your feelings by yelling or expressing them in an angry tone. Continue to do that until you feel better.

2.   Write an affirmation. Examples:

I, _____, *forgive myself and I am okay.*

I, _____, *am a good person and I deserve success.*

3.   If it is appropriate, write a letter of apology to someone you feel you have wronged, even if they are deceased. Mail it or throw it away. You may also call the person, or meet with them to apologize.

Parents' Approval

We may push away success if we are afraid that our parents will be jealous of us. The following exercise will help you overcome this block to success.

1.   Allow yourself to close your eyes and take two deep breaths.

2.   Imagine that you are asking each parent separately if you can be more successful and happier than they are or were.

3. Hear them, or imagine them, saying, "Yes."
4. If either or both parents say, "No," then imagine nurturing parents who support you to be all that you are.
5. Do the Grounding Cord process and take two deep breaths.
6. Write an affirmation: I, _____, am successful and my parents love me.

Letting Go

In this exercise, you will imagine yourself being as successful as you choose to be. Some examples are: having a healthy, slim body; enjoying prosperity, a loving relationship and a fulfilling career; being a successful artist, singer, or musician; and living in a new house. Then you will get in touch with what you may need to let go of before you are willing to be that successful image.

1. Allow yourself to close your eyes and take two deep breaths.
2. Visualize or sense yourself reaching your goal.
3. How do you look? Where are you? What are you doing? How are you feeling?
4. Now say to the successful image, "In order to become you, I need to let go of the belief that _____" and finish the sentence.
5. If you are ready to let go of that negative belief, imagine that you are writing it on a piece of paper, ripping it up and throwing it away.
6. Take a deep breath.
7. Now imagine that you are writing a positive thought with a colorful magic marker and putting it somewhere you will see it often. (Examples: your wallet, refrigerator, or bathroom mirror.)
8. Repeat this process (numbers 4-7) until you feel complete.
9. Now imagine that you are blending and becoming one with your success image. How are you feeling?
10. Visualize or sense how your life will be different. How are you feeling?

11. Do the Grounding Cord process and take two deep breaths.
12. Open your eyes and write down your affirmations.

Visualize your goals

What we visualize, or imagine is what we are likely to attract to us. This process can assist you to create your life as you choose it to be.

1. Close your eyes, relax, and take a few deep breaths.
2. Visualize or imagine your life the way you desire it to be.
3. Say to yourself, "All this and more is coming to me easily and effortlessly."
4. Do the Grounding Cord process and take two deep breaths.

Treasure Map

This fun and empowering exercise can help you actualize all your goals. We attract to us what we say, think, feel and imagine. Therefore, putting all that information on a poster board can help us ground all our goals into reality. Examples: a healthy, slim body, happy relationships, abundance, a new home or car, a successful career and fun vacations.

1. Write down your goal: Example:
   I am earning $75,000 plus a year.
2. List all the things you want to do with your earnings. Examples:
   Live in a nice two-bedroom condo
   Vacation two weeks in Hawaii
   Purchase a new white van
   Take dancing lessons
   Donate money to a good cause
3. Cut pictures out of magazines, or draw your own, to illustrate what you want and paste them on poster-board. Make sure that it is the exact thing you want, including the color. Include your affirmations. Hang it up where you can see it often. Examples:

A photo of you next to the car (exact model, year and color) you desire
A picture of you slim and happy with your friends and family
A picture of where you want to vacation
A photo or drawing of your home

Congratulations on being willing to face your blocks to success and overcome them. If you are still not actualizing your goals, you may want to repeat all or some of the exercises. The following affirmations can also assist you to enjoy the success and happiness you deserve.

Affirmations to Overcome the Fears of Success

Here are some affirmations for the Seven Major Fears of Success. It is helpful to put your name in the blank space. Put a <u>check</u> next to the affirmations you would like to focus on.

1. Fear of the Unknown

___1. I, _____, have the courage to experience new people and things.
___2. I, _____, am taking risks, because I choose to feel satisfied with my life.
___3. I, _____, am ready to face the unknown.
___4. I, _____, trust myself to be able to deal with new situations and people.
___5. I, _____, am scared and I have the courage to do what I want.
___6. I, _____, am visualizing the way I want my job and/or relationship to be, and I am allowing myself to move on.

2. Fear That Success Does Not Fit My Self-image

___1. I, _____, am imagining a positive image of myself.
___2. I, _____, am seeing myself with an abundance of money and love.
___3. I, _____, am imagining myself thin, healthy and happy.

___4. I, _____, am seeing myself as a confident, intelligent person.

___5. I, _____, accept my new, successful image of myself.

___6. I, _____, am a successful person.

3. Fear That I Do Not Deserve Success

___1. I, _____, am beginning to believe that I might deserve to be happy and successful.

___2. I, _____, am beginning to believe that I deserve to have an abundance of money and love.

___3. I, _____, forgive myself for all my mistakes.

___4. I, _____, deserve success in my relationships and my career.

___5. I, _____, accept that it is my birthright to be happy and successful.

___6. I, _____, am allowing myself to be happy and loved.

4. Fear That People Will Not Like Me If I Am Successful

___1. I, _____, am successful and people are happy for me.

___2. I, _____, am successful and I have many friends.

___3. I, _____, am meeting people who support my success.

___4. I, _____, am modeling success and happiness and I am loved and safe.

___5. I, _____, am successful in my career and I am in a loving relationship.

___6. I, _____, am happy and people who want to feel good are attracted to me.

5. Fear That Success Has a Scary Consequence

___1. I, _____, am wealthy and I am a good, caring person.

___2. I, _____, am rich and people want to be with me because they like me.

___3. I, _____, am successful and I have enough time for myself and my loved ones.

___4. I, _____, am in a loving relationship and I am free to be me.

___5. I, _____, am slim and safe.

___6. I, _____, am attractive and I can handle the attention I receive.

6. Fear That My Parents Will Not Love Me If I Am More Successful Than Them

___1. I, _____, am more successful than my parents and they love me.

___2. I, _____, am more successful than my mother and she is happy for me.

___3. I, _____, earn more money than my father and he is very pleased.

___4. I, _____, accept that I can be happier and more successful than my parents because opportunities are so much better now.

___5. I, _____, accept that my parents love and support me to be all that I am.

___6. I, _____, accept that my parents want me to be happy and successful.

7. Fear That to Be Successful Is to Fulfill My Parents' Ambitions

___1. I, _____, am successful, because I choose to be.

___2. I, _____, accept that my parents did the best they could with the information that they had.

___3. I, _____, am fulfilling my ambitions.

___4. I, _____, am focusing on being all that I am.

___5. I, _____, forgive my parents for all their mistakes.

___6. I, _____, love and accept my parents.

Now that you know how to make affirmations, you can also write your own. Say, sing, or write your positive thoughts until they become part of your automatic thinking. If you are still not actualizing your goals, it may be because you have more fears to resolve, or it is not the right time, what you really want, or for your highest good. Be preserving and remember that you do have the power to attract what you desire.

Chapter 21

Raising Self-Esteem

With a high self-esteem, you are more likely to allow yourself to actualize your personal and professional goals. This exercise can help you raise your self-esteem.

1. Say to yourself, or write down on a piece of paper:
   I rate my self-esteem as a _____ (fill in a number from 1–10, 10 being the highest).
2. Now write: In order to raise my self-esteem I want to _____ (finish the sentence). Continue to say the sentence until you record all of your thoughts. Examples:
   I want to be more patient with others.
   I want to be more accepting of myself.
3. Then write: In order to raise my self-esteem I need to _____ (finish the sentence). Again keep writing until you feel complete. Examples:
   I need to stop comparing myself to others.
   I need to talk to someone about my problems.
4. If you are willing to do those things to raise your self-esteem, then write out the details and a plan of action. It may also be appropriate to write affirmations. Examples:
   I, (your name), am more patient with others.
   I, _____, accept myself.
   I, _____, appreciate who I am and what I can do.
   I, _____, am asking a counselor for help.

"Loving Yourself"

It is important to like and love yourself in order to allow yourself to be happy and successful.

Hold a soft, cuddly pillow, or stuffed animal in your arms. Close your eyes and relax. Imagine that the pillow or stuffed animal is you and hold it close. Say to yourself: You, (your name), are okay. You are a good person. I like you. I love you. You deserve success and happiness.

Chapter 22

A Healthy Body

The truth is that we are very powerful beings. We have the ability to create our illnesses or accidents as well as our health and safety. In order to be healthy and full of vibrant energy, it is helpful to understand that our physical bodies express our thoughts and feelings. We can take an active part in healing ourselves when we listen to what our bodies are telling us, constructively express our emotions and resolve our issues. We can experience optimum safety, health and happiness. The following information and exercises can assist you in your healing process. *

Identifying Feelings

Your feelings are expressed in your body. Therefore, by tuning into where you feel tension or pain, you can discover how you are feeling.

Put a <u>check</u> next to the body parts that you feel tension, pain, or have problems with.

A. I have a condition or illness, or I feel pain or discomfort in my:
___1.   Stomach
___2.   Abdominal area
___3.   Thighs
___4.   Lower legs

___5. Throat
___6. Heart
___7. Genitals
___8. Feet

Note: You may be feeling **afraid**.

B. I have a condition or illness, or I feel pain or discomfort in
    my:
___1. Forehead
___2. Temples
___3. Jaws
___4. Cheeks
___5. Arms
___6. Teeth (from grinding)
___7. Back
___8. Hands
___9. Center of back of neck
___10. Shoulder blades

Note: You may be feeling **anger**.

C. I have a condition or illness, or I feel pain or discomfort in
    my:
___1. Sinuses
___2. Right and/or left side of the back of my neck
___3. Sternum (center of the chest)

Note: You may be feeling **sadness**.

D. I have a condition or illness, or I feel pain or discomfort in:
___1. Both sides of the back of my neck
___2. Heart

Note: You may be feeling **hopeless**.

E. I have the following symptoms:
___1. Dizziness
___2. Nausea
___3. Vomiting
___4. Weakness

___5. Body feels cold
___6. Blurry vision
___7. Faintness
___8. Numbness
___9. Can't breathe
___10. Labored breathing
___11. Speechless
___12. Hyperventilation

Note: You may be feeling **extreme fear**.

Body Messages

The body is very literal. Tension in a certain area may be caused by a specific negative thought. When you identify what your body is trying to tell you and change the thought to a positive one, you are likely to experience relief.

Put a <u>check</u> next to the symptom (pain or pressure) you have. (Note the example of what you may be thinking.)

___1. Band across the forehead – *"I'm holding myself back."*
___2. Eyes – *"I don't want to see ___."*
___3. Ears – *"I don't want to hear ___."*
___4. Whole neck – *"Somebody or something is a pain in the neck."*
___5. Throat – *"I am afraid to say ___."*
___6. Line across the back of the neck – *"I don't want to feel."*
___7. Shoulders – *"I feel responsible for ___."*
___8. Spine – *"I don't have the backbone."*
___9. Chest – *"I feel stifled, suffocated." "I am holding back."*
___10. Heart – *"I have a broken heart."*
___11. Hands – *"I don't know what to do." "I cannot handle it." "I feel helpless."*
___12. Genitals – *"I'm feeling vulnerable, so I am closing down." "I won't let people in."*
___13. Hip – *"I'm afraid I won't survive."*
___14. Backside – (Can be interpreted as: sitting on feelings or pain from being spanked.) *"Someone or something is a pain in the backside."*
___15. Knees – *"I cannot stand on my own two feet."*
___16. Legs – *"I want to run away."*

___17. Feet Moving – *"I want to kick someone or something."*
___18. Cold feet – *"I'm scared." "I'm afraid to get angry or hurt someone."*
___19. Feet off the ground – *"Part of me does not want to be here."*
___20. Toes curling – *"I want to leave* (earth).*"*
___21. Tingles in any part of the body—if it feels good it can mean you are letting go of tension; if it feels bad it can mean that tension is still there.

Now that you know how you may be feeling and/or what your negative thought may be, continue to the next exercise to deal with your emotions so that you can feel good.

Dealing With Feelings

The following exercise can help you overcome your negative feelings so that you can feel good, relaxed and expanded.

1. Take three deep breaths.
2. Notice where you feel tension, or pain in your body. If there is more than one, pick the area where it is the strongest first.
3. Identify what you may be feeling in that area by the above lists. I feel _____.
   (Examples: sad, angry, afraid, etc.)
4. Express your feeling a few times to bring it to the surface and release it. It is helpful to say it congruently (your words and tone match). For example: Say, *"I'm sad,"* in a low, sad voice.
   "I feel _____."
   "I feel so _____."
   "I feel so _____."
5. Find out the cause of your feeling by adding the word *because*. For example, *"I am feeling sad because I didn't get the job that I wanted."*
   I feel _____ because _____.
   If you need to express your feelings to someone (it may be yourself too), write a letter and decide if you want to send it or not.

Dear _____

I know that I'm responsible for all my feelings. I want to tell you that I feel _____ *because*

_____.

Thank you for hearing me.

6. You are finished with the exercise when there is no more tension in your body.

Congratulate yourself for dealing with your feelings in a healthy way and taking an active part in healing yourself.

"Note: This information is not to replace medical care.

Chapter 23

Healthy Sexuality

The following HART exercises can help you to get in touch with and release any issues that you may have concerning your sexuality.

If you are under professional care, before you work with these exercises I recommend that you discuss these issues with your mental health provider. They may trigger an upsetting past experience, and it is wise to have some support ready, in case you need it.

I am pleased to have this opportunity to assist you to overcome your sexual issues. You deserve to fully enjoy your normal, healthy sexuality.

Sex Questionnaire

Check off the following beliefs that you relate to:

___1. People want to be with me only for sex.
___2. I feel too vulnerable when I am sexual.
___3. I feel I have to perform for my partner.
___4. I feel pressured to have an orgasm to please my partner.
___5. I feel guilty for enjoying my sexuality.
___6. If I initiate sex, my partner will feel I am too aggressive.
___7. If I enjoy sex too much, men will think I am loose.
___8. I am afraid of becoming addicted to sex.

The beliefs that you checked off indicate negative sexual thoughts that can be blocking you from enjoying your sexuality. You may want to repeat the questionnaire after you work with the following exercises.

Sex Means to Me

1. Say or write the words: Sex means to me _____. Fill in your negative answer. Example: Sex means pain.
2. Now let go of that fear-based decision by crossing it off, or deleting it.
3. Then change that negative thought to an all-positive one. Example: Sex means feeling good.
4. Repeat numbers 1-3 until you only associate sex with positive thoughts. Continue to write, say, or sing your affirmations until they become part of your automatic thinking.

Overcoming Resistance to Your Sexuality

1. On one piece of paper, write down your specific goal concerning your sexuality. Example: I enjoy my sexuality.
2. Then write, *I can't* _____ (fill in your goal) because _____.
   Continue to say the above sentence and write down and number all of your negative thoughts until you feel complete.
3. On a second piece of paper write, I *won't* _____ (fill in your goal) because _____.
   Continue to say the above sentence and write down all of your negative thoughts until you feel complete. These are the negative thoughts that are keeping you from enjoying your sexuality.
4. On a third sheet of paper, make an affirmation for each negative thought. Examples:
   Negative Thought: *I can't be sexual because I am a bad person.*
   Affirmation: *I, (your name), believe that I am a good person, and I deserve to enjoy my sexuality.*
   Negative Thought: *I won't be sexual, because men use me.*

Affirmation: *I, (your name), am sexual with men who care about me.*

5. Then throw out the pieces of paper with your negative thoughts. Keep only the affirmations and continue to say them until they feel part of your automatic thinking.

Visualize Your Goals

1. Close your eyes, relax and take a few deep breaths.
2. Visualize yourself enjoying your sexuality.
3. Say to yourself, "I am enjoying my healthy sexuality."

How are you feeling now? Are you open to expressing your healthy sexuality? If you still feel negative about sex, I suggest that you work with the other exercises in this section until you reach your desired results.

Chapter 24

Effective Parenting

We often learn how to parent from how we were parented. Even if we did not appreciate some of the ways we were treated, we are likely to unconsciously repeat the same negative behavior with our children. Sometimes we go to the other extreme, and that is usually not helpful.

For example, if your parents were too strict, you may be too lenient. The healthy way is to have appropriate boundaries and guidelines.

The following exercise can help you be more aware of your parents' modeling and how you are parenting. The insights can assist you to be a more successful parent.

My Parents Modeling

1. Write down on a piece of paper: I *liked* that my mother _____. Keep writing down all the thoughts that come to you. Example: I liked that my mother was affectionate, happy and caring.
2. Put a check next to all the things that you also do as a parent. If there is a healthy behavior that you liked, but are not doing, you may want to consider being that way with your child.
3. Do the same process with your father. I *liked* that my father ___. (Repeat #'s 1 & 2.)

4. Now write the following: I *did not like* when my mother
    _____. Keep writing down all the thoughts that
    come to you. Example: I *did not like* when my mother
    yelled, or had no time for me.
5. Now put a check next to all the things that you also do
    as a parent. If there are some behaviors that you did not
    like, but you are doing them with your child, you may
    want to change your behavior to be more loving and
    constructive. Example: I am speaking calmly and
    spending quality time with my child.
6. Do the same process with your father. I *did not like*
    when my father _____. (Repeat #'s 4 & 5.)

Are you now more aware of how you are parenting? I
suggest that you continue to be conscious of your behaviors that
are not working well and replace them with actions that are
more effective. Then you can enjoy your role with your child and
reap the benefits of seeing him or her happy and successful.

Chapter 25

Truths Set You Free

*I*n the process of my self-healing and service to others, I have learned to listen to and be grateful for my internal guidance, my intuition. This is how the 101 truths came to be. One morning, I woke up and my first thought was to begin to write definitions. Feeling inspired, I went to the computer and the definitions flowed from my fingers. When I read the 101 truths through, I realized that the insights came from my heart, my work with clients, my intuition and my own inner healing journey.

Therefore, I recognize that these definitions are subjective. You, as the reader, may have a different opinion. I encourage you to add, or edit what feels right to you. However, I do advise you to keep the definitions all positive. In other words, say what the truth is instead of what it is not. I also suggest that if you create your own truths, make them specific, and let them help you clarify your beliefs, feel good to you, and inspire you to experience more success and happiness in your life. The more conscious you are of what you are thinking, the more you will be able to create the life you desire.

1. ABUNDANCE is allowing myself to have all that I desire and all the goodness that life offers me.

2. ACCEPTANCE is a precious gift I give to myself and others.

3. ADDICTIONS are anything I do in excess in an attempt to run away from or numb my pain.

4. AGGRESSION is angrily demanding what I want.

5. ANGER is covering up underlying feelings of fear, hurt, or powerlessness.

6. ASSERTION is asking unconditionally for what I want.

7. BALANCE is taking the time to work, play and be quiet.

8. BEAUTY is what I can choose to see in everyone and everything.

9. BEHAVIOR is an outward expression of what I am thinking and feeling.

10. BODIES are to be nurtured and cared for as temples of our souls.

11. CARING is kind words, thoughts and actions.

12. CHILDREN are individuals who need to follow their own unique paths.

13. COMMITMENT is an agreement that I intend to fulfill and to communicate if I choose to change.

14. COMMUNICATION is sharing my thoughts and feelings unconditionally.

15. COMPASSION is an acceptance and appreciation of a thought, feeling, or experience in another or myself.

16. CONFLICT occurs when there is non-acceptance of another's perceptions.

17. CONFUSION is felt when two or more parts of me are telling me opposite things.

18. CONTROL or manipulation is what I may do when I am scared.

19. COURAGE is doing something even though it is scary.

20. DECISIONS are best made from my intuition, my inner wisdom.

21. DISAPPOINTMENT is what I feel when I think people, or events should be different.

22. DOUBTS are what I feel when I do not trust others or myself.

23. EMOTIONS are determined by my positive or negative thoughts.

24. EXCITEMENT is doing what I love.

25. EXPERIENCES depend on how I perceive them.

26. FAITH is trusting and believing in myself, others and a higher source.

27. FEAR is often based on the mistaken belief that I am not okay.

28. FLOWING is effortlessly doing what appears to be working.

29. FORGIVENESS is important for me to do for others and myself.

30. FREEDOM is seeing my choices and acting on them.

31. FRIENDS are people who accept, respect and appreciate me.

32. FRIENDSHIPS are people sharing life's joys and challenges.

33. FULFILLMENT is how I feel when I am true to myself and doing what I love.

34. GIVING is an unconditional expression of my caring.

35. GOALS are guidelines that offer me direction.

36. GOOD ENOUGH is a feeling that I have no matter what other people say or do.

37. GUILT is a mistaken belief that I have to do something in order to be okay.

38. HAPPINESS is accepting and loving myself and feeling peacefully powerful.

39. HARMONY is being in tune with others and myself.

40. HEALING is learning and accepting that I am good enough, worthwhile, important, lovable, intelligent and attractive, and that I deserve to be happy, healthy and successful.

41. HEALTH is living from love and expressing and balancing my mind, body, emotions and spirit.

42. HEARTS are designed to be open, to allow love to flow in and out.

43. HONESTY is realizing and expressing what I am thinking and feeling.

44. HUGS are a wonderful way of telling people I care.

45. HUMOROUS is when all parties are laughing.

46. ILLNESS is my body telling me that I am thinking negative thoughts and not expressing my feelings.

47. IMPORTANT is a feeling of being valued for who I am.

48. INDEPENDENT is relying on myself for my needs and decisions.

49. INNER PEACE is my greatest contribution to world peace.

50. INTUITION is my inner wisdom guiding and protecting me.

51. JEALOUSY is believing I am not good enough.

52. JOY is how I feel when I follow my heart and my dreams.

53. JUDGMENTS are negative thoughts that can hurt others and me.

54. LIFE is a wonderful journey to be lived to the fullest.

55. LISTENING is hearing and accepting people's perceptions.

56. LOVABLE is allowing myself to express my love.

57. LOVE is a feeling of deep caring—it is what makes me feel truly alive.

58. MARRIAGE is a loving partnership between equals who are best friends.

59. MINDS are magnificent computer-like machines that are programmable.

60. MISTAKES offer me opportunities to learn.

61. MONEY is wonderful to give and receive, and a tool to help build dreams.

62. MORALITY is based on what I believe in my heart.

63. NATURE is a reminder of how to simply be.

64. PAIN is believing that I am not okay, good enough, worthy, important, lovable, attractive and intelligent, or that I am responsible for the problems of others.

65. PATIENCE is having faith that everything is perfect as it is.

66. PEACEFUL is a feeling of contentment for being who I am.

67. PEACEFUL POWER is feeling that I am okay and I am free to be me.

68. PLAY is one way I have fun, release tension and re-energize.

69. POTENTIAL consists of my capabilities, which are most valuable when I express them.

70. POWER is fulfilling my potential and helping others to do the same.

71. PRESENT is being totally in the moment, a key to happiness and success.

72. PRIDE is pretending not to feel vulnerable, scared, or hurt.

73. PROBLEMS are opportunities for me to find win-win solutions.

74. PRODUCTIVE is doing things that make a difference to others or myself.

75. PROSPERITY is my birthright.

76. PROVING or performing is trying to convince others and myself of my value.

77. RECEIVING is feeling worthy and allowing another the gift of giving.

78. RELATIONSHIPS are an opportunity for me to give and receive unconditional love.

79. RESENTMENT is thinking that what a person did means that I am less than okay.

80. RESPECT is acknowledging someone's innate value.

81. RESPONSIBILITY is realizing that I am in charge of my life.

82. SAFE is realizing that my positive thoughts and actions are my protection.

83. SECRETS are hidden thoughts that may keep me separate from others.

84. SELF-LOVE is a deep knowing that I am okay and that I deserve to be happy.

85. SERVICE is anything I do from caring that helps others.

86. SPACE is what I sometimes need to be quiet and gather my thoughts.

87. SPIRIT is my unlimited, all knowing and unconditionally loving self.

88. SPIRITUAL is acting from my spirit (love) and supporting others to do the same.

89. STRENGTH is being able to do what I need to do to feel good.

90. STRESS is what I experience when I am feeling fear instead of love.

91. SUCCESS is an internal feeling of fulfillment, peace, and power that comes from being who I am, and doing what I truly want to do.

92. TALENTS are my unique gifts that want to be expressed.

93. THOUGHTS are my decisions based on my experiences.

94. TRUST is believing that others and I will do what we say.

95. UNCONDITIONAL LOVE is an expression of my acceptance and deep caring.

96. WHOLENESS is feeling that I have everything inside of me to make me happy.

97. WINNING is allowing myself to be all that I am.

98. WISDOM is a knowing that love and acceptance are always the solution.

99. WORK is what I do to serve others and myself.

100. WORLD PEACE is possible when we see everyone as sisters and brothers — as one global family.

101. WORTHY is feeling that I deserve all that I receive.

HART Trainings and More Inspirational and Educational Materials

With the goal of assisting as many people as she can, Helene Rothschild has written the following inspirational, empowering, and self-help educational materials:

An online interactive self-help program: "Personal Success"
Online E-books (also read out loud)
Books and Booklets
Tapes
Posters
Cards
Articles (note free ones on her website)

Helene also offers international teleclasses, and independent studies and trainings in the HART process.

For more information call: 1-888-639-6390

helene@helenerothschild.com
http://www.helenerothschild.com

About the Author

Helene Rothschild MS, MA, MFT, Marriage, Family Therapist, was born in Brooklyn, New York, USA. She received a Bachelor and Master's Degree in Science in Health and Physical Education at Brooklyn College and taught at Lafayette High School for six years.

In 1976, she moved to California and earned a Master's degree in Marriage, Family & Child Counseling at the University of Santa Clara, in Santa Clara, California. After Helene became licensed, she founded and directed the Institute for Creative Therapy, a non-profit educational counseling center. In addition to counseling clients, she trained and supervised other therapists in a process she developed, called Creative Therapy (HART).

Helene has also shared her unique ideas with hundreds of audiences and facilitated many self-help workshops. She hosted her own local radio and television shows and appeared numerous times in the media, including on the international Cable News Network (CNN).

Helene's mission is to help as many people as she can "love themselves to peace," which she believes is the key to health, happiness, and success, and the greatest contribution to world peace. She has touched millions of people internationally with her inspirational and self-help articles, books, e-books, tapes, cards, and posters.

Helene has committed her life to service. She has the courage to listen to and follow her intuition. In 1993, her inner wisdom motivated her to move to Sedona, Arizona. In 1997, she was the founder and CEO of Joyful Living, a non-profit educational organization. The mission is also to assist people to experience love and peace. Through Joyful Living, she has donated thousands of her educational materials to other non-profit organizations.

In 2003, Helene moved to Carmel Valley, California. Since January 2005, she has been traveling internationally. She continues to serve many people, through her phone sessions, classes, workshops, lectures, media appearances, and educational materials.

Helene has raised two children and she has four grandchildren. She loves to have fun, dance, hike, network, and explore different places.